Contents

Pupil Book 3

Charlie and Ben Move House

Ben is Charlie's special friend, but only Charlie can see him.

Rat-tat-tat!
Charlie jumped out of bed in his Super Mario pyjamas. Ben was already at the window, wearing the same pyjamas. Ben was Charlie's special friend. They always dressed the same. In fact, they could almost be brothers. Rat-tat-tat!

From six floors up, they watched the man from the Estate Agents bang the last nail into the "Sold" sign outside the block of flats. Ben kicked the skirting board. He had a habit of kicking things when he wasn't happy.

"At least we'll have a bigger room in the new place," said Charlie.

"Who needs a bigger room?" said Ben stubbornly.

"No more climbing up all those stairs to get to our flat," said Charlie.

"What's wrong with stairs? We have marble races on the stairs," said Ben grumpily.

"We'll have a garden instead of a balcony," said Charlie.

"I like balconies," said Ben. "You get to throw things off balconies."

That was true, thought Charlie. No more of his favourite game, Bombs Away! Dropping bags of flour out of the window, seeing whose would hit the courtyard and explode first. Charlie kicked the skirting board, but forgot he wasn't wearing any shoes. "Ow!" he cried. Ben could kick anything he liked and never hurt himself. But then, Ben was different.

"What are you up to, Charlie?" asked Mum. She stood at the door with a letter in her hand looking cheerful.

*from **The Moving Mystery***
by Carmen Harris

Charlie's special friend

Read the extract on page 2, then answer these questions in complete sentences.

The easy way to answer questions in complete sentences is to use the words in the question to start you off.

Who was Ben? Begin your answer: **Ben was …**

A
1. Who was Ben?
2. What woke Charlie up?
3. What did Ben do when he wasn't happy?
4. Why was he unhappy?
5. What will Charlie and Ben miss when they move house?

B
1. Why do you think Ben never hurt himself when he kicked anything?
2. Why do you think Mum was looking cheerful?
3. What do you think will happen next?

Writing sentences

A Copy these sentences, but remember to use capital letters and full stops in the right places.
1. charlie jumped out of bed
2. he had a friend called Ben
3. they always dressed the same
4. mum stood at the door
5. she had a letter in her hand

All sentences begin with a capital letter.
Most sentences end with a full stop.

B Write three sentences about yourself. Don't forget the capital letters and full stops.

C
1. Write three sentences about your home.
2. Write three sentences about your school.

Our house

A Read this description of the house in the picture. Think for yourself what the missing words and phrases are.

Our house is semi-detached. The Thompson family live next door. Our house is painted _____ with a _____ front door. There is _____ window downstairs and _____ upstairs. Our front garden has a small _____ and a cherry _____. In spring the tree is full of _____ blossom and looks very _____. We have a garage at the side with a _____ door. We never put the car in because it is full of tools, _____, _____, _____ furniture and a _____ machine. I like living here because _____.

B Write a description of your home or a house you know well. Use the description above to help you plan yours. First write a list of suitable words and phrases which will make your description real.

Question marks

This is a question mark: **?**
Questions always end with a question mark.

A Rewrite these questions, remembering the capital letters and question marks.
1. who needs a bigger room
2. what is wrong with stairs
3. where are we moving to
4. when was Charlie woken up
5. how did Charlie hurt his foot
6. why is Ben different

B Questions usually begin with a question word:

Why? What? Who? Where? When? How?

Write six questions of your own. Begin each sentence with a different question word.

C Make up five questions of your own about your classroom.

An Exciting Letter

Jo has sent an invitation to the Mayor to judge her Best Kept Gerbil Competition. Now a letter has arrived from the Town Hall.

Jo read her letter again, just to make sure. *Dear Ms Johnson*, it began. That had fooled Jo at first; she had never been addressed as Ms Johnson before, only Jo. *The Mayor has asked me to write to you and thank you for your invitation to judge your Best Kept Gerbil Competition. He will be delighted to perform this honour at 6pm on Thursday 2 August, at 35 Victoria Road, Clagthorpe. Yours sincerely, V Simpkins (Miss) Personal Secretary to The Mayor.*

PS. The papers and the TV will be there, too.

Annabelle lived at the top of a block of flats, and Jo arrived flustered and breathless.

"We're in the lounge," said Annabelle.

Annabelle's flat was huge and bright, with a smashing view of Clagthorpe. The gang were all sitting on the floor in a circle, in the middle of which Annabelle's two gerbils, Trish and Phipps, were playing with an old cornflakes packet. In the far corner sat a little old lady. In front of her was a large television set, which she was watching out of the corner of one eye. On her lap was a newspaper, which she was reading out of the corner of her other eye. On the table beside her was a radio, which she was listening to, and on her lap was a long brightly-coloured scarf, which she was knitting.

"Don't mind Gran," said Annabelle.

Jo sat down and told the gang the good news about the Mayor. Well, she didn't so much *tell* them, as shout at them over the noise of the telly and the radio.

"Magic!" yelled Leslie.

"Brilliant!" yelled Javinder.

"Wow!" yelled Annabelle.

from **Philomena Hall and the Best Kept Gerbil Competition** *by Roy Apps*

Jo's letter

Day 1

Read the extract on page 5, then answer these questions in complete sentences.

A

1. What was exciting about Jo's letter?
2. Who would be coming, besides the Mayor?
3. What sort of competition was being held?
4. What did Jo do when she had read the letter?
5. How did her friends react to the news?

B

1. What is Jo's last name? How do you know?
2. Explain fully what Granny was doing.
3. What do you think will happen next?

S,W
Day 2

The things people say

In cartoons spoken words are put inside **speech bubbles**.

In stories spoken words are put inside **speech marks**.

" goes before the first word that is spoken.

" goes after the last word that is spoken.

Look at the pictures and complete these sentences by using the words from the speech bubbles.

1.

" _____," said Jo.
" _____?" asked Annabelle.

2.

" _____!" cried Jo.
" _____," replied Annabelle.

3. Do the same with these sentences, but add your own speech marks.

_____,
announced Jo.

_____, said Javinder.

Words ending in -le

Look at these words ending in **-le**:

table	candle	circle	little	rattle
middle	handle	bottle	jumble	cradle

Choose one word from the list for each space in this passage.

The children were sitting in a ___1___ in the ___2___ of the floor. They were playing with a ___3___ doll lying in a ___4___. On a ___5___ was a ___6___ of things. There was an empty ___7___, a melted ___8___, an old door ___9___ and a baby's ___10___.

Describe your living room

Use the description of Annabelle's flat on page 5 to help you write a description of your own living room.

Draw a sketch, or a plan, of the room to get things clear in your mind.

Make a note of the things you will put in your description, like this:

General impression (size, colours, brightness, etc.)
medium size – bright colours – sunny

View from window
small garden – tree – houses

Furniture and soft furnishings (curtains, carpet, etc.)
green carpet – patterned curtains – table

People (who they are, what they are doing)
brother, playing with toy cars

Ending (what you feel about your living room)

Words ending in -ing

A Many words that end in **-t**, **-p** or **-n** double the last letter when adding **-ing**.

sit + ing = sitting
hop + ing = hopping
run + ing = running

1. Add **-ing** to these words. Don't forget to double the last letter.
   a) knit
   b) drop
   c) bat
   d) win
   e) sip
   f) hit
   g) fan
   h) slip
   i) fit
   j) skip
2. Choose five of the words above and use each one in a sentence of your own.

B Words ending in **-e** usually drop it before adding **-ing**.
invite + ing = inviting
judge + ing = judging

1. Add **-ing** to these words. Don't forget to drop the final **e**.
   a) welcome
   b) hope
   c) prepare
   d) stare
   e) live
   f) scrape
   g) smoke
   h) wade
   i) type
   j) tease
2. Choose five of the words above and use each one in a sentence of your own.

The School Bell

Story-teller:	It was playtime at Park Road Primary School and Miss Cross was on duty.
Miss Cross:	Come along, children. Get off that wall. It's not safe.
Kate:	Yes, Miss Cross.
Miss Cross:	And stop teasing the little ones.
Ali:	We weren't teasing them, Miss Cross. They keep following us.
Miss Cross:	Well, be nice to them, then.
Grant:	We are.
Miss Cross:	That's enough from you, Grant!
Grant:	But …
Story-teller:	Miss Cross gave them all one of her looks and they started to walk away.
Miss Cross:	Oh, Ali. You can do a job for me.
Ali:	Yes, Miss Cross.
Miss Cross:	Go and get me the bell, will you?
Ali:	Where is it, Miss?
Miss Cross:	On the shelf outside Mrs Sorter's office.
Story-teller:	Ali went in to get the bell.
Kate:	Is it nearly time, Miss Cross?
Grant:	Shall we line up?
Miss Cross:	Yes.
Story-teller:	Ali came running back.
Ali:	It's not there, Miss Cross.
Miss Cross:	Are you sure?
Ali:	I couldn't see it anywhere.
Miss Cross:	But it must be.
Story-teller:	Just then, Mrs Sorter walked across the playground.
Mrs Sorter:	You look worried, Miss Cross. Is anything the matter?
Miss Cross:	Oh, Mrs Sorter. I am glad you've come. The bell seems to be missing.
Grant:	You had it last playtime, Miss Cross.
Kate:	I know because I took it back for you.
Ali:	But it's not there now.
Mrs Sorter:	Let's go and look. I'm sure it can't be far away.
Story-teller:	The children and Miss Cross went with Mrs Sorter.

from **The School Bell** *by Jacquie Buttriss and Ann Callander, Collins*

Day 1 The bell is missing

Read the extract on page 8, then answer these questions in complete sentences.

A

1. Who was on duty in the playground?
2. What did she stop the children from doing? Why?
3. Who was cheeky to Miss Cross?
4. Where was the school bell kept?
5. Why did Miss Cross look worried when Ali came back?

B

1. Who do you think Mrs Sorter is? What makes you think so?
2. What do you think might have happened to the bell?
3. What do you think will happen next?

Day 2 Exclamation marks

An exclamation mark is a kind of exciting full stop. It may be used for commands, warnings or threats. It is also used to show surprise:

> I don't believe it!

A Finish these sentences with exclamation marks:
1. Go away
2. The winner is … Ali
3. Come back
4. Don't open the door
5. Not one more word, or else

B Write five exclamations of your own. Don't forget the exclamation marks!

Different kinds of sentences

A Find and write down one example each of a statement, a question, an order and an exclamation from the play extract on page 8.

B Put exclamation marks or question marks where they are needed in the following sentences:
1. I never thought I'd win
2. What time is dinner
3. Look out
4. That hurt
5. Oh no, it's raining
6. When are you coming back
7. Do it now
8. Have you finished
9. What a beautiful picture
10. May I help you

C Write two statements and two orders of your own.

How does the story end?

Write your own ending to the playscript of *The School Bell*.
Here is the cast of characters that you can use:

Story-teller

Miss Cross

Kate

Ali

Grant

Mrs Sorter

As there are only six characters, one of them
must have taken the bell. Who is most unlikely to have done so?

Why do you think one of the others has taken it?

What might he or she have done with it?

How will Mrs Sorter find that person? What questions might she ask?

How will she get the bell back?

Write down your ideas as a story plan. Then begin your playscript like this:

Scene: Outside Mrs Sorter's office

Miss Cross: It should be here on this shelf.

Mrs Sorter: Don't worry, Miss Cross. I expect someone is playing a
trick on us.

Story-teller: She turned to face the children.

About me

A Write six interesting statements about yourself.

B Write six interesting questions to which you would like to know the answers.

C Collect examples of exclamations, statements, questions and orders from
your reading.

Unit 4

A Cage for a Mouse

Grandad has found an old cage and brought it home.
Chris wants a mouse, and his sister Mary is waiting
to see his reaction when he spots the cage.

She hears the back gate crash against its latch. Chris is home from school. He ambles in and throws down his bag, helps himself to a mug of tea and tips back on his chair. Mary waits for him to spot the cage.

"What's that?" he asks at last.

"Your grandad found it," says Mum.

"Cor, great," says Chris, examining it. "Now I can get my mouse."

"Oh no, you can't. I'm not having vermin in this house."

"But Mum …"

"And that's final."

"Go on, Mum. It's only a mouse. White mice aren't vermin. You ought to see Ben's. They don't smell, honest."

All week he talks about mice.

He straightens the bars on the cage and scrubs it out. And Grandad makes a little door and fixes it on with wire.

"Please, Mum. I'll keep it in the shed. You won't even see it. Mice are nice when you get to know them …"

"I'll give you mice if you don't shut up!" Mum threatens.

"Great!" he yells. "Then I'll go on, and on, and on, and on …" He ducks the tea-towel that she throws at him.

Mary knows he'll get his way: somehow he always does.

from **The Trouble with Mice** *by Pat Moon*

Day 1 Chris wants a mouse

Read the extract on page 11, then answer these questions in complete sentences.

A

1. Where did the cage come from?
2. What did Chris say to persuade his mum to let him have a mouse?
3. Why did Mum say he couldn't have one?
4. Who helped him repair the cage?
5. What did Mary think about Chris?

B

1. What do you think "vermin" are?
2. Explain why Chris said he would go "on and on, and on, and on …"
3. What do you think will happen next?

Day 2 Verbs

A Choose a verb from the words below for each of these pictures.

walk drink swim play run read eat write watch listen

> Verbs are action words. They tell us what people do.
> Chris **helps** himself to a cup of tea and **tips** back on his chair.

B Write a sentence of your own about each of the pictures above.

C Write a list of six action words for things you do each day. Use each one in a sentence of your own.

Different ways of speaking

There are many different verbs for ways of speaking.

Complete these sentences with suitable verbs from the words below.

whispered promised shouted
laughed replied asked exclaimed

1. "Where are you going?" she _____.
2. "To the shops," he _____.
3. He _____ to his friend so that no one else would hear.
4. "What a fantastic idea!" _____ Kuldip.
5. He _____ over the noise of the machinery.
6. "You do look funny!" _____ Ginny.
7. "I'll be on time," she _____.

Mum, I want a pet!

Dialogue is conversation in books or plays. In plays, the speaker's name is always written on the left, and there is a space before the spoken words. Each speaker begins a new line.

Chris: What's that?

Mum: Your grandad found it.

Have you ever tried to persuade parents to let you keep a pet? What did you say? Did you get your pet? Write a playscript about what happened, or what you think might happen if you asked for one now.

Plan your ideas for each part of the conversation like this:

The beginning
What pet did you want? How did you ask for it? What did your parent(s) say at first?

The middle
What did you say to persuade them? What promises did you make?

The ending
Did you get your way? What did you say at the end?

Prefixes: dis- and un-

A **prefix** is a group of letters that you add to the beginning of a word to make a new word.

dis + appear = disappear   **un** + happy = unhappy

dis + agree = disagree   **un** + fasten = unfasten

A Make opposites by adding the prefix **dis-** or **un-** to these words. You can leave out the hyphen. For instance, **un-** + tie = untie.

1. tidy
2. like
3. fair
4. do
5. trust
6. honest
7. dress
8. pack
9. sure
10. obey
11. comfortable
12. approve

B Use each of the new words you have made in a sentence of your own to show what it means.

C Think of some more **un-** or **dis-** words. Make a list for each prefix.

Walking the Goldfish

Harry is complaining that he is bored.

His father stood it for a few minutes. Then he said: "Harry, sit down! You're driving me mad. And I want to watch this video in peace."

"But I'm *bored*," answered Harry.

"You can't be! You've got books and TV and all your friends in the village. You've got everything any boy needs to be happy and interested in life. It's *impossible* for you to be bored."

"It's not impossible, and I *am* bored."

His dad gave a deep groan and switched his gaze from the video. Fingering his moustache, he glanced round the room and spotted the goldfish bowl. "Look," he said, pointing, "look at Cleo. What about her, eh? Now, she has every right to be bored. Nothing to do all day but swim round and round that bowl. Never sees anything new, unlike you. She's the one you ought to feel sorry for, Harry, not yourself."

"I *do* feel sorry for her," said Harry, jumping up to make faces at his goldfish again. But she didn't seem a bit interested in what he was doing, "especially if she's as bored as I am. But what can I do about it?"

"Oh, *I* don't know – take her for a walk, or something." His dad grinned, but with his eyes still fixed on the screen.

Harry was suddenly delighted. "Do you mean it, Dad? Can I really take Cleo for a walk?" He began to plan where they might go in the village.

"I said so, didn't I? Go on, get off with you – then you'll both stop being bored." The video was showing pictures of funny-looking, flat-topped cars whizzing past each other like super-fast ants.

Harry wondered how to carry Cleo on her walk.

*from **Walking the Goldfish** by Michael Hardcastle*

Harry's bored!

Read the extract on page 14, then answer these questions in complete sentences.

A
1. Why did his father think it impossible for Harry to be bored?
2. Why did he think Harry should be sorry for the goldfish?
3. What did Harry do to interest the goldfish?
4. What did his dad suggest Harry should do?

B
1. Do you think Harry's dad was serious about walking the goldfish? What makes you think so?
2. Why do you think he made the suggestion?
3. Do you think Harry took his suggestion seriously? Give a reason for your answer.
4. How would you go about taking a goldfish for a walk?

Doing the opposite, doing the same

A Change the verbs in these sentences to an opposite meaning.
The first one has been done for you.
1. John **hates** baked beans.   *John **loves** baked beans.*
2. They **pulled** the heavy box into the room.
3. As it was late he decided to **go**.
4. They **played** all afternoon.
5. She **whispered** a warning.
6. When she heard the news she **laughed**.

B Change the verbs in these sentences so the meaning is the same.
The first one has been done for you.
1. She **noticed** that the shop was closed.   *She **saw** that the shop was closed.*
2. The thief **snatched** her bag.
3. The magician waved his wand and the ring **vanished**.
4. **Pick** any book you like.
5. He **ate** his dinner quickly.
6. He **stumbled** over a stone as he **ran** down the hill.

C Use these verbs in sentences of your own:

sail   look   chew
show   lift   open

D Think for yourself what the missing verbs are in this further extract from *Walking the Goldfish*. Choose one word for each space.

Harry wondered how to carry Cleo on her walk. She ___1___ in a very large, heavy bowl that was hard enough just to ___2___. Then, in the kitchen, he ___3___ the see-through jug they ___4___ Cleo in when they ___5___ the water in her bowl. It ___6___ very big but it was easy to ___7___ because it ___8___ a handle. Harry ___9___ to himself as he always ___10___ when he had a bright idea.

A home for a pet

A Write a description of how you would set up a cage for a gerbil, a guinea pig or a mouse. First read the instructions on the opposite page for setting up an aquarium. Use these instructions as a model for your own writing.

Make notes of your ideas under these headings.

The cage
How big is it? What is it made from? What features does it have?

Preparing the cage
What will you need to put in it, such as bedding, food and water containers, toys?

Food
How will you feed and water your pet?
What kind of food will it need? How often?

Cleaning the cage
How often will you need to clean out the cage? What will you do with your pet while you are cleaning?

B Continue this picture story with your own pictures showing what happens when Harry takes his goldfish for a walk. Write some spoken words for each picture.

"Take the goldfish for a walk".

Setting up an aquarium

Never keep a goldfish in a bowl. Instead use a fish tank, where there is a greater surface of water open to the air.

Tanks
There are many kinds of aquarium, but a plastic tank is ideal for a single goldfish. It should measure at least 45 cm × 30 cm × 30 cm. Place a layer of washed gravel in the bottom to a depth of about 5 cm.

Plants
Plants add oxygen to the water. Choose suitable cold-water plants, and bury the roots in the gravel, weighing them down with washed stones.

Filling the tank
Cover the gravel and plants with a sheet of paper to prevent them being washed out as you fill the tank with water. Remove the paper and leave the water for 24 hours before you add the fish.

Day 5 · Verbs: past and present tenses

Many verbs make their past tense by adding **-ed**:

    sail – sailed rest – rested pick – picked play – played

Some verbs change in other ways:

    go – went see – saw catch – caught take – took is – was

Present tense verbs tell us what is being done now: He **walks**.
Past tense verbs tell us what has already been done: He **walked**.

A Change the verbs in these sentences into the past tense. Do it like this:

School starts at nine o'clock.
School **started** at nine o'clock.

1. I play the violin.
2. The shops close at six.
3. She opens the door.
4. He keeps a goldfish in a tank.
5. He takes it for a walk.
6. They go to town.
7. He digs the garden, and then cuts the grass.
8. Paul sits, but Tom stands.

B Change these verbs into the past tense and use them in sentences of your own.

1. plant
2. look
3. turn
4. fill
5. see
6. kick
7. burn
8. fly
9. run
10. blow
11. buy
12. go

Unit 6

The Senses

Jigsaw Puddle

Sloshing my boat in the pavement puddle
I jiggle the sky above,
I fold the clouds in a sheep-like huddle,
I bobble the sun in the blue and white muddle –
And then I stand still –
Till the jigsaw puddle
Is smooth as a mirror again.

Emily Hearn

Ice Cream and Fizzy Lemonade

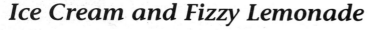

Ice cream is sliding, soft and cold
And gives a smooth and soothing coat
On hot summer days
To the back of your throat.

Fizzy lemonade looks like water
But as you unscrew the bottle top
Bubbles crowd together in froth
With a rushing sound and a sudden pop.

It prickles and tickles your nose
And tingles the back of your throat
That needs another sliding soft ice cream
To give it back a smooth and soothing coat.

Stanley Cook

Smells

I like the smell of brand-new shoes
The scent of sweet new hay;
The steamy smell of ironing
At home on washing day.
I love the tang of ocean,
And the petrol smell of cars;
But I hate the smell of cigarettes,
And Uncle Bill's cigars.

A. Elliott-Cannon

Sounds

The whistling of the wind,
The pattering of the rain,
The tapping of the hail-stones
Upon the window-pane.

The splashing of your gum-boots
In the puddles of the lane.
The gurgling of the water
As it rushes down the drain.

The cooing of the pigeon,
The crying of the eagle,
The snorting and the sniffing
And the barking of the beagle.

The slam of a large door,
The slam of a small,
The crack of a rifle,
The bounce of a ball.

The very very quiet sounds –
The walking of some ants;
The very very noisy sounds –
The run of elephants.

Alexander Kennedy

Sounds and smells

Read the poems on page 18, then answer these questions.

A

1. Find words from the poems which rhyme with these: puddle, coat, pop, lane, ball, rain.
2. Which words tell what it is like to drink fizzy lemonade?
3. Find two loud and two soft sounds in the poem "Sounds".
4. Which smells does the poet **not** like in "Smells"?

B

1. What do you think these words mean: jiggle, bobble, tang?
2. Explain the title "Jigsaw Puddle".
3. Which poem do you like best? Why?

Words that mean the same

A **thesaurus** is a book that lists words with similar meanings. Use a thesaurus to help you choose more interesting words.

Synonyms are words that have the same or nearly the same meaning:

It was a **wet** day. It was **rainy** weather. His clothes were **soaked**.

A Copy these sentences, replacing **wet** with a more suitable or interesting word.
1. He wiped it clean with a **wet** cloth.
2. Today the weather will be **wet**.
3. He was **wet** in the thunderstorm.

B Replace the word **big** in these sentences.
1. The box was too **big** for me to lift.
2. The elephant is a **big** animal.
3. The school grounds were **big**.
4. I have one **big** sister.

C Replace the word **hard** in these sentences.
1. This puzzle is too **hard**.
2. The seat was **hard** to sit on for very long.
3. The over-cooked meat was very **hard**.
4. Digging the garden is a **hard** job.

D Find at least five synonyms for these words:

cold   hot   small   thin   beautiful

E Make sentences of your own with five of the synonyms you have found.

Writing a list poem

The poems "Smells", "Sounds", "The Feel of Things" and "What is Red?" are list poems. The poets have selected an interesting list of ideas, and carefully arranged them to make a poem.

Use one of their poems as a model for your own list poem. Choose one of these titles:

Sounds (or Smells) I Love
The Feel of Things
What is Yellow? (or another colour of your choice)

This is a good way to go about writing a list poem:

Planning
Brainstorm words and ideas about your subject. Think of how it feels, looks, sounds, smells or tastes. What do you particularly like about it? Make a list of your ideas.

Choose interesting words to bring your ideas to life. Use a thesaurus to find synonyms.

Drafting
Select your most interesting words and ideas. Sort them to make an interesting poem.

Revising
Read your poem aloud, perhaps to a friend. How can it be improved?

Make changes to your poem. Read it through again, and make further changes if you need to.

Proofreading
Check your draft for spelling and punctuation mistakes.

Presenting
Write your final draft in your best handwriting, or use a word processor.

20

The Feel of Things

I like roughness in warm towels
Smoothness in cool sheets;
I like to feel the stinging rain
Needling on my cheeks.
I like to feel soft bedroom rugs
When my feet are bare.
I like the new-washed silkiness
Of our baby's hair.

A. Elliott-Cannon

What is Red?

Red is a sunset
Blazing and bright.
Red is feeling brave
With all your might.
Red is a sunburn
Spot on your nose.
Sometimes red
Is a red red rose.
Red squiggles out
When you cut your hand.
Red is a brick
And the sound of a band.
Red is hotness
You get inside
When you're embarrassed
And want to hide.
Fire-cracker, fire-engine
Fire-flicker red –
And when you're angry
Red runs through your head.
Red is an Indian,
A Valentine heart.
The trimmings on
A circus cart.
Red is a lipstick
Red is a shout
Red is a signal
That says: "Watch out!"
Red is a great big
Rubber ball.
Red is the giant-est
Colour of all.
Red is a show-off,
No doubt about it –
But can you imagine
Living without it?

Mary O'Neill

Describing things

Adjectives describe nouns:

fizzy lemonade   **stinging** rain   **blazing** sunset

A   Sort these adjectives into the five senses.
The first ones have been done for you.

soft	blue	fragrant
sweet	loud	enormous
prickly	musty	sour
rough	round	smooth
silent	scented	deafening
bright	perfumed	quiet
bitter	salty	

Sight	**Touch**	**Taste**	**Smell**	**Hearing**
blue	soft	sweet	fragrant	loud

B   Make a list of suitable adjectives to describe these things:
a fizzy drink
a rose
a firework
the sea

Find adjectives for as many of the senses as you can.

C   Write one or two sentences
describing each of the items above.

D   Choose three things to describe
in sentences of your own.

Diwali

Diwali (or sometimes Divali) is the Hindu festival of light.

Diwali is a Hindu festival and the themes of Diwali tell us about what Hindus believe. Hinduism centres around the worship of God, who can be worshipped in different ways through different Hindu gods. The most important thing for a Hindu is to love and please God – by living a good life, by setting up shrines at home, by frequent prayers and by celebrating the many Hindu festivals. Diwali is such a festival.

Diwali is the Hindu festival of light. The word Diwali is short for dipawali, which means "row of lights". Diwali is celebrated during late October or early November, when it gets dark early and the nights are cold, long and dark. Hindus enjoy preparing for festivals as much as they enjoy celebrating them. They can start preparing for Diwali a month before the festivities begin and the celebrations can last for up to five days.

At Diwali, the dark nights are lit up. Houses have welcoming lamps at all their doors and windows, and multicoloured lights decorate the streets. The temples are covered with tiny rows of lights and the sky is ablaze with fireworks. Shop windows are piled with different-coloured sweets and everybody wears their brightest clothes.

Diwali is celebrated for different reasons all over India because different gods are honoured in different areas. However, all the different Diwali festivities have a lot in common. They celebrate the triumph of good over evil, light over darkness, life over death. It is a time of hope and new beginnings.

*from **Diwali** by Kerena Marchant*

Traditional clay lamps, called diwas, are placed at doors and windows throughout the festival of Diwali.

Day 1 The festival of light

A Read the extract on page 22, then copy and complete this passage about Diwali.

Diwali is a Hindu _____. The word Diwali means _____ of lights. Diwali is celebrated when it it gets _____ early, and the nights are cold, _____ and dark. Diwali celebrations can last for up to _____ days. At _____ the houses have lamps in their _____ and windows. The _____ are covered with tiny rows of _____. Fireworks light up the _____. Everybody _____ their brightest clothes.

B Answer in complete sentences. Look for the **emphasised** key words in the passage.
1. What are **diwas**?
2. What do **all the different Diwali festivities** have **in common**?
3. Why do you think Diwali takes place **when it gets dark early**?

W

Day 2 I got a nice surprise!

Read this story:

I **got** quite a surprise this morning. I had just **got** my breakfast when the doorbell rang. The postman had **got** a parcel for me. I don't **get** many parcels so I **got** quite excited. I **got** it open and found I had **got** a present from Uncle Tom. He said he would **get** me a radio-controlled car, and there it was. I **got** out of the washing up and **got** it working right away. I **got** on the phone and asked my friend if he would like to **get** over and play with it. He **got** on his bike and **got** here in no time. "I wish I had **got** one of those," he said.

Now read this:

I received quite a surprise this morning. I had just sat down to breakfast when the doorbell rang. The postman had a parcel for me.

A Rewrite the first passage above, replacing **got** and **get** with a better word or phrase.

B Rewrite the following passage, replacing **nice** with a better word or phrase.

It's **nice** to be on holiday, especially on a **nice** day. We were staying at a **nice** hotel in a **nice** seaside town. The food was **nice** and the hotel staff were all **nice**. We had a **nice** day on the beach. In the evening we had a **nice** walk and looked at all the **nice** lights. We certainly had a **nice** time.

The lights are bright at night

Look at the words ending in **-ight** in these sentences.

At **night**, during Diwali, the streets are **bright** with coloured **lights**.

Complete these sentences with a suitable word ending in **-ight**.
1. I can't unscrew this jar. The lid is too _____.
2. Bats fly at _____.
3. Take care with that knife or you _____ cut yourself.
4. I watched him until he was out of _____.
5. It is wrong for people to _____.
6. It was a calm day with just a _____ breeze.

23

A list of festivals

This is the contents page for a book on festivals.

A

1. Which chapter would you read if you wanted to learn about these?
   a) The Feast of St Lucia
   b) West Indian Carnival
   c) Id-ul-Fitr
   d) Chinese New Year
   e) Christmas
   f) Festive recipes
   g) Diwali
   h) Hannukah

2. Which page number would you turn to for information on these festivals?
   a) Id-ul-Fitr
   b) Feast of St Lucia
   c) Christmas
   d) Diwali
   e) West Indian Carnival
   f) Chinese New Year
   g) Hannukah

B

1. Name one of the recipes you might find in Chapter 8.
2. Write a few lines describing your favourite festive food.

Days 3 and 4

Describe a festival you know

Festivals are great fun, and there are many different kinds: Chinese New Year, Christmas, Diwali, Hannukah, Id-ul-Fitr, West Indian Carnival.

Write about a festival you know well. Make notes of your ideas. Use your notes to write three paragraphs, telling a friend about your chosen festival.

Plan your work like this:

Introduction
What does the festival celebrate?

When and how often does it take place?
Why does it take place at this time?

How it is celebrated
Think of the sights, sounds, smells and tastes of the festival.

What can you say about these special things: customs, decorations, food, clothes, music?

What other special things happen at this time?

Ending
What do you particularly enjoy about this festival?

The Flat Man

At night when it is dark
and I am in bed
and I can't get to sleep
I hear noises.

I hear tap, tap, tap.
I know what it is.
It's a tree blowing in the wind.
It taps on the glass.
That's all.

But I like to pretend
it's The Flat Man trying to get in.
His long, bony finger
taps on the glass.

"Let me in," he whispers.
Tap, tap, tap.

I like scaring myself.
It's only a game.

I hear rattle, rattle, rattle.
I know what it is.
A train is going by.
It makes the whole house shake
and the windows rattle,
as if its teeth are chattering.
That's what it is.

But I like to pretend
it's The Flat Man squeezing himself
as thin as he can
through the crack.

"You can't keep me out," he whispers.
Rattle, rattle, rattle.

I hear shsh, shsh, shsh.
I know what it is.
It's my baby brother
making noises in his sleep.
It sounds as if the sea's coming in.

But I like to pretend
it's The Flat Man
sliding around the room.
"I'm coming," he whispers.
Shsh, shsh, shsh.

He keeps his back
close against the wall.
He clings like
a stretched out skin.
And I know why.

I know The Flat Man's secret.
He's afraid of the light.
He hates open spaces.
That's why he creeps in corners
and drifts in the dark.

One flash of bright light
and he would shrivel up
like a crumpled piece of paper.
The slightest breeze
could blow him away.

So he slips and slides
in the shadows
until he is near my bed.
Then silently
he waits for his chance.

from **The Flat Man** *by Rose Impey, Collins*

I like to pretend …

Read the extract on page 25, then answer these questions in complete sentences.

A

1. What game does the boy play?
2. What sound does he pretend is the tapping of bony fingers?
3. What sound does he pretend is The Flat Man sliding around the room?

B

1. What is The Flat Man's secret?
2. Why do you think the boy plays this kind of game?
3. What do you think will happen next?

Now and then

This extract from *The Flat Man* is written in the **present** tense, as if it is happening now.

I **hear** rattle, rattle, rattle. I **know** what it **is**.

We can change these verbs into the past tense:

I **heard** rattle, rattle, rattle. I **knew** what it **was**.

A Rewrite the following extract. Change the **bold** verbs into the past tense.

It **makes** the whole house shake and the windows rattle, as if its teeth are chattering. That's what it **is**.
But I **like** to pretend it **is** The Flat Man squeezing himself as thin as he **can** through the crack.

B Do the same with these sentences:

He **keeps** his back close against the wall. He **clings** like a stretched out skin. And I **know** why. I **know** The Flat Man's secret. He **is** afraid of the light. He **hates** open spaces. That is why he **creeps** in corners and **drifts** in the dark.

C Do the same with this passage:

I **pull** the covers up and **hold** them tight under my chin. This **is** to stop The Flat Man from creeping into bed with me …
I **lie** there afraid to move. An icy feeling **is** spreading all the way up my back. Someone or something **seems** to be wrapping itself around my chest. I **can't** breathe!

D Change these verbs into the past tense and use them in sentences of your own.

dry catch sing bring
go drink eat draw
write sweep

At night when it is dark …

Write a story of your own using the opening sentence of *The Flat Man* to start you off:

At night when it is dark and I am in bed and I can't get to sleep I hear noises.

Plan your work like this:

Planning
What noises do you hear?

What do they make you think of?

How do you feel?

Writing
Write your story in four paragraphs.

Paragraph 1:
What is the first noise you hear?

What do you pretend it is?

How does it make you feel?

Paragraph 2:
Answer the same questions for a second noise.

Paragraph 3:
Do the same for a third noise.

Paragraph 4:
How does it all end?

Do you fall asleep? Call for help? Or does something else happen?

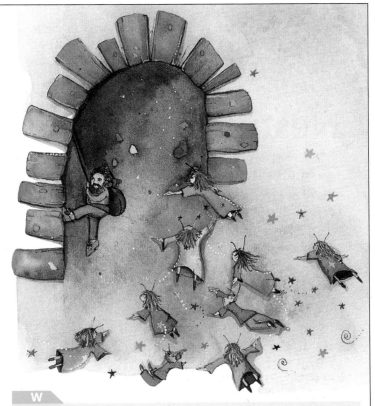

Prefixes: pre-, de- and re-

pre- means "before": so "prefix" means a group of letters placed before a word to make a new word.

de- changes the meaning of a word to its opposite: activate – deactivate

re- means "again": rebuild – to build again

A
1. Make new words by putting **pre-**, **de-** or **re-** before these words.
   a) historic
   b) frost
   c) tend
   d) play
   e) place
   f) mist
   g) arrange
   h) view
   i) code
   j) fresh

B Write a sentence of your own for each word you have made.

Nesting Birds

The nesting season is a time of great activity for all birds. First they have to find a place where they can build their nests and feed. This area then becomes their territory. When they have found a mate they have to build a nest, lay eggs and rear their young. With all this going on, it is not difficult to find out when and where a bird is building its nest or feeding its young. A bird carrying something in its beak is the most common sign.

The Song Thrush builds its nest in a bush. There are usually four or five eggs. Both parents feed the young birds with worms and snails.

When a parent bird approaches the nest, the young birds beg for food with wide, open mouths.

The adult bird arrives at the nest with food. It pushes the food into the mouth of one of the young birds, removes any droppings from the nest and flies off to collect more food.

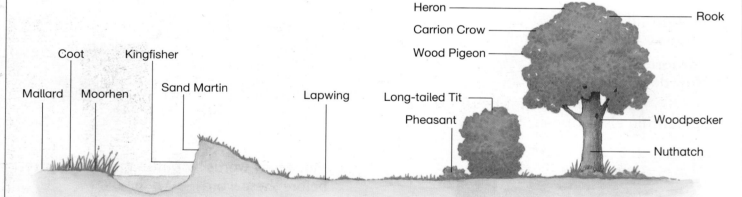

Coot   Kingfisher

Mallard   Moorhen   Sand Martin   Lapwing

Heron   Rook
Carrion Crow
Wood Pigeon

Long-tailed Tit   Woodpecker
Pheasant   Nuthatch

In the country, birds nest in many different places. They use trees and hedges, the shelter of steep banks and holes in trees.

Some birds, like the Lapwing, make hardly any nest at all. They lay their eggs in a shallow hole in the ground.

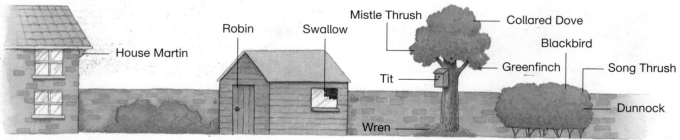

House Martin   Robin   Swallow

Mistle Thrush   Collared Dove
Blackbird
Tit   Greenfinch   Song Thrush
Wren   Dunnock

Many birds nest in gardens but only in sheltered places, safe from cats and dogs. They use thick bushes, trees, ivy-covered

walls and sheds as well as nesting boxes. Some birds, like the House Martin, even build under the roof.

from **The Nature Trail Book of Birdwatching**

About nesting birds

A Look on page 28 for the answers to these questions.
1. Where do these birds nest?
   a) house martin
   b) woodpecker
   c) lapwing
   d) blackbird
   e) kingfisher
   f) collared dove
2. Which birds nest in the tops of trees?
3. Which birds nest on the ground?

B Answer in complete sentences.
1. What is the most common sign that a bird is building a nest?
2. What happens when a parent bird approaches the nest?
3. What name do we give to the place where birds build their nests and feed?

Days 2 and 3

Presenting information as a chart

A **chart** is way of presenting information in rows and columns.

A Use the diagrams on page 28 to help you complete the chart below.

Bird	Trees	Hedges	Ground	Holes in banks	Sheds and houses
Blackbird		✔			
Carrion Crow		✔			
Collared Dove	✔				
Coot			✔		
Dunnock					
Greenfinch					
Heron					
House Martin					
Kingfisher					

Add these birds to your chart:

Long-tailed Tit Moorhen Song Thrush Tit
Lapwing Nuthatch Swallow Woodpecker
Mallard Pheasant Robin Wood Pigeon
Mistle Thrush Sand Martin Rook Wren

B Make two lists: one should list all the birds which nest in trees, and the other should list all the birds which nest in hedges.

Using diagrams

Diagrams are a way of giving information in pictures and words.

A Look at the diagram on page 28, which shows where birds nest. Draw your own labelled diagram to show which birds nest in trees.
a) Draw the outline of a tall tree.
b) Bring together the birds which nest in trees in the country and which nest in trees in gardens.
c) Add labels to your outlines, listing the birds which nest in the tall tree.

B Make a diagram to show which birds nest in hedges.

Clues to meaning

When we read, we often come upon a word which is new to us. If we read the whole sentence carefully, we can pick up clues to the meaning of the new word.

What do you think the **bold** words mean in these sentences? Read the whole sentence carefully.
1. Many birds live here during the summer, but **migrate** when the weather gets cold.
   a) go to sleep
   b) fly to another country
   c) build a warm nest

2. Most birds spend the day looking for food, but at night they **roost**.
   a) eat the food
   b) sing
   c) settle down for the night

3. Wild birds live in many different **habitats**, such as fields and hedges, woods and mountains.
   a) places where they live
   b) trees
   c) nests

4. The long-eared owl is **nocturnal**, but also hunts by day.
   a) a hunting bird
   b) active at night
   c) active during day and night

5. Rooks are **gregarious** birds, building their nests together in rookeries.
   a) enjoying living together
   b) fine nest builders
   c) greedy

Making notes by using key words

We call the most important words in a passage the **key words**. They are the keys that unlock the main points of the passage.

In the paragraph below, the first few key words are **emphasised**. Notice that short, unimportant words are left out.

The **nesting season** is a **time of great activity for all birds. First** they have to **find** a **place** where they can **build** their **nests** and **feed**. This area then becomes their territory. When they have found a mate they have to build a nest, lay eggs and rear their young. With all this going on, it is not difficult to find out when and where a bird is building its nest or feeding its young. A bird carrying something in its beak is the most common sign.

1. Make notes by writing the key words, like this:
   Nesting season – time of great activity for all birds. First find place – build nests, feed.
2. Complete your notes by picking out the remaining key words and writing these down too.
3. Read all the words you have picked out. Even though they will not make complete sense they should give you the main points of the passage.

Bird spotting

Wren 9.5 cm
The smallest garden bird. Brown with a tilted-up tail.

Goldcrest 9 cm
The smallest European bird. Dull green. The male has a bright yellow/orange crest.

Blue tit 11.5 cm
Blue and white head, yellowish underparts and blue-grey above.

Robin 14 cm
One of our best-loved birds. Orange breast. Younger birds are brown and speckled.

Dunnock 14.5 cm
Feeds on the ground. Brown above, grey beneath.

Chaffinch 15 cm
Male is brown above, white bars on the wings and a pink breast. The female is smaller and duller in colour, without the pink breast.

A ·Use the information from this page and from page 28 to help you copy and complete this chart.

Bird	Size	Appearance	Where it nests
Blackbird	25 cm	Male: black with yellow beak Female: dark grey-brown	Hedges
Blue tit			
Chaffinch			
Dunnock			
Goldcrest			
Robin			
Wren			

B Write two or three sentences about each of the following birds, using information from this page and from page 28:

a) wren **c)** robin
b) blue tit **d)** dunnock

Write about their size, their appearance and where they nest.

Unit 10

Shape Poems

one

t
hi
s

snowflake

(a
li
ght
in
g)

is upon a gra

v
es
t

one

E. E. Cummings

Sky Day Dream

WITH THEM

COULD FLY OFF

I WISHED THAT I

INTO THE SKY

FLY OFF

SOME CROWS

ONCE I SAW

Robert Froman

Mosquito

Mozzie

Marie Zbierski

Snake

Snake glides
   through grass
     over
       pebbles
         forked tongue
     working
    never
speaking
    but its
      body
        whispers
         listen.

Keith Bosley

Calligrams

A **calligram** is a word written in a way which matches its meaning.

A calligram can be a word written in a **shape** to show its meaning:

Some words can be used to make **pictures** which represent their meanings:

A Write each of the following words in a shape to show its meaning:

fat, stretch, falling, climbing, growing, splitting, curved, tall

B Make a picture from each of these words to represent its meaning:

cold, shivering, bang, earthquake, fast, drip, crash, bright

C Make calligrams of these opposites: big – small, thick – thin, wide – narrow, steady – shaky

Ancient
Modern

Using a thesaurus

A Find the word **move** in a thesaurus. Choose six suitable synonyms to make into calligrams.

B Find other words in a thesaurus or dictionary to make into calligrams.

Calligram sentences

Complete sentences may be written as calligrams.

Write each of the following sentences in a way that represents its meaning.

1. The roller coaster climbed up, paused for a moment, hurtled down and up again, and once more down, before coasting to a stop.
2. When I got off the roller coaster I was shaking all over.
3. The music got louder, and louder, and louder.
4. When it's time for bed I go up the stairs as slowly as I can.

Write your own shape poem

Look at the poems on page 32, then write a shape poem of your own using one of these ideas.

a rocket   a butterfly   a snake   spaghetti

a flower   a tree   a train   a lollipop

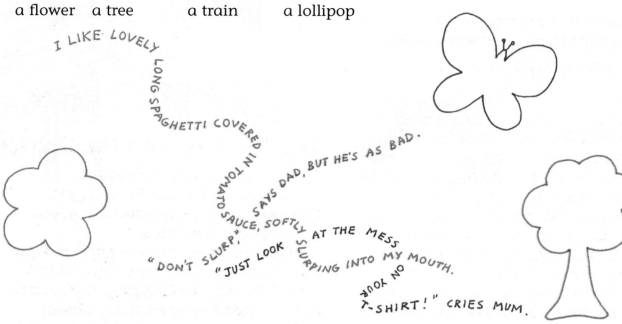

I LIKE LOVELY LONG SPAGHETTI COVERED IN TOMATO SAUCE, SOFTLY SLURPING INTO MY MOUTH. "DON'T SLURP," SAYS DAD, BUT HE'S AS BAD. "JUST LOOK AT THE MESS ON YOUR T-SHIRT!" CRIES MUM.

This is a good way to go about writing a shape poem:

a) Choose a subject.

b) Draw a shape to suit your poem.

c) Make a list of interesting words and sentences about your subject.

d) Write your poem in rough.

e) Check your poem carefully. Does it say all you want it to say? Are there any spelling mistakes? Is there any other way it could be improved?

f) Make your changes.

g) Copy out your poem in your best writing in the shape that you drew earlier.

More calligram sentences

Write calligram sentences using these ideas and some of your own.

1. a kite at the end of a long line
2. the flight of a paper aeroplane as it swoops and glides before landing
3. a diver walking along a diving board and diving into the water, the last word representing a splash
4. a conversation between two people represented as telephone wires strung between telegraph poles

Unit 11

Fables

A fable is a short story which usually has animals as its characters and teaches a "moral" or lesson.

The Foolish Crow

A crow perched on the branch of a tree, holding in his beak a piece of meat. Before he could eat it a fox saw him and decided that he wanted the meat for himself. He stood under the tree and began to tell the crow what a handsome bird he was.

"With your looks," said the wily fox, "you should be king of the birds and you certainly could be if your voice was as impressive."

The crow was so keen to prove that he had a good voice that he opened his beak and croaked for all he was worth. The piece of meat fell to the ground, where the fox quickly gobbled it up and said, "And if you added brains to all your other qualities, you'd make a first-class king."

MORAL
Vanity is the mark of a fool.

from Aesop's Fables

The Greedy Dog

A dog was crossing a river with a piece of meat in his mouth. He saw his reflection in the water and thought it was another dog carrying what looked like a bigger piece of meat than his own. Straight away the dog dropped his meat and made a grab for the larger piece. Of course, he ended up with nothing, for his own piece was swept away by the river and the other was just a reflection.

MORAL
Greedy people end up with less.

from Aesop's Fables

The Sparrow and the Ostrich

The ostrich said to the sparrow, "You must obey me. I am bigger, stronger and more important than you who are almost nothing."

At that moment, hunters appeared and saw the ostrich. They took aim and in a second the ostrich was dying. The sparrow flew away and escaped. Being almost nothing, the hunters took no notice of him.

from Fables from Africa, retold by Jan Knappert

The Persistent Dog

A dog was trying to crack a thigh-bone between his teeth. "Why all that trouble for a hard old bone?" asked his master. The dog answered, "I hope to find some soft marrow inside."

from Fables from Africa, retold by Jan Knappert

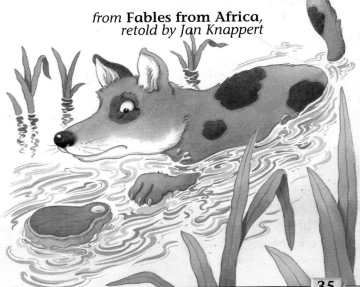

Understanding fables

Read the fables on page 35, then answer these questions in complete sentences.

A
1. In what way was the crow foolish?
2. What did the greedy dog try to get?
3. Why did the hunters take no notice of the sparrow?
4. What did the persistent dog expect to find in the bone?

B
1. In what ways are these fables similar?
2. What do you think are the morals of "The Sparrow and the Ostrich" and "The Persistent Dog"?
3. Which fable did you like best? Give a reason for your answer.

Plurals: -es

When words end with the letters **s, x, z, sh** or **ch,** we add **-es** when making the words plural:

   one fox, two fox**es**

   one dish, three dish**es**

   one watch, two watch**es**

A   Change these words into their plural forms.
1. match
2. bus
3. dish
4. buzz
5. box
6. kiss
7. stitch
8. peach

B   Rewrite these sentences, changing the **bold** words to plural. Notice that you may also need to change other words. The first one has been done for you.
1. I saw a **fox**.   *We saw some* **foxes.**
2. The **box** was put on the **coach**.
3. He made a **wish**.
4. I am eating a **peach**.
5. **He** is striking a **match**.
6. **She** wants to go to the **church**.
7. **She** threw a **six**.
8. I fell in the **ditch**.

Suffixes: -er, -est

A **suffix** is a group of letters added to the end of a word to make a new word.

Two common suffixes are **-er** and **-est**:
   quick, quick**er**, quick**est**
   slow, slow**er**, slow**est**

Many words ending in a consonant double the consonant before adding the suffix.
   big, bi**gg**er, bi**gg**est
   sad, sa**dd**er, sa**dd**est

A   Complete the following. The first one has been done for you.
1. cold, *colder, coldest*
2. warm, _____ _____
3. sad, _____ _____
4. fast, _____ _____
5. green, _____ _____
6. fat, _____ _____
7. narrow, _____ _____
8. fit, _____ _____

B   Complete these sentences.
1. The dog with the big piece of meat saw another dog with a _____ piece.
2. Mr A is strong, Ms B is _____, but Mr C is _____ of all.
3. I am tall, my friend Kelly is _____, but Jan is the _____.
4. Ravi can run fast. He is the _____ runner in school.

Make up your own fable

A fable is a short story, usually with animal characters, which teaches a moral lesson.

Make up your own fable. Use one of the fables on page 35 as a model. Think of how you might change the story, perhaps using different characters or a different setting.

Here are some ideas for you to consider.

Settings
Choose a setting for your fable: a wood, a field, a stream, a farm, or somewhere else.

Characters

wolf   fox   hen   dog   cat   mouse   lion   snake

Plan what will happen in your story. You can do this by making notes or drawing pictures.

Look at the way fables begin and end. Start and end **your** fable in a similar way.

Suffixes: adding -y

> We can make new words from other words by adding the suffix -y.
> rain + **y** = rainy
> snow + **y** = snowy
> wind + **y** = windy

1. Make new words from these words by adding -**y**:
   frost   cloud   rust
   Use each one in a sentence to show its meaning.

2. When a word ends in a silent -**e** we drop the **e** before adding -**y**.
   ice + **y** = icy
   shine + **y** = shiny
   stone + **y** = stony
   Make new words from these words by adding -**y**:
   noise   taste   ease
   Use each one in a sentence to show its meaning.

3. With many short words we double the last consonant before adding -**y**.
   sun + **y** = sunny
   fog + **y** = foggy
   run + **y** = runny
   Make new words from these by adding -**y**:
   slip   mud
   spot   chop
   nut   fun
   nip   chat
   dot   tin
   Use each one in a sentence to show its meaning.

Wolf Tales

The Rabbit and the Wolf

This is a traditional tale from Turkey.

One day when a rabbit was walking in the forest, he heard someone crying out, "Help! Help!" He looked around, and finally he saw a wolf. A great stone had fallen on his back so that he could not get up. He asked the rabbit's help, and said that he would die if nobody helped him.

The rabbit worked very hard, and finally managed to get the big stone off the wolf's back. Then the wolf jumped up and caught the rabbit in his mouth. The rabbit cried and asked for pity, but the wolf insisted on killing him for his meal.

Then the rabbit said, "No good person kills someone who has helped him. It is not fair. You can ask the duck, who is very fat and knows everything."

So both of them went to the duck. He listened to their story and then he said,

"Show me the stone." They went to the stone.

"Now, let me be sure about this," said the duck. "Put the stone on the wolf's back exactly as it was when you found him." So the wolf lay down, and with much effort the stone was put on his back again.

"Well, what do you think?" said the wolf to the duck.

The duck thought for a moment. Then he said, "I think you were wrong to be cruel to the rabbit, who had helped you. Now see if someone else will help you!"

And leaving him in the sorry state in which the rabbit had come upon him, they went their way.

*from **Turkish Folk-tales**,*
retold by Barbara K. Walker

Getting the story straight

These pictures show the beginning, middle and end of the story of "The Rabbit and the Wolf" on page 38.

A Copy out in the correct order the following sentences about the story:

The duck said that the stone should be put back on the wolf.

The rabbit said this was unfair and that they should ask the duck what to do.

A rabbit came and freed the wolf, but the wolf said he would eat the rabbit.

They left the wolf under the stone to see if someone else would help him.

A wolf cried for help to free him from a stone which had fallen on his back.

When this was done the duck said the wolf was cruel to the rabbit.

B Draw the three missing pictures from the picture story on the left. Write a sentence of your own for each picture.

Is and are, was and were

We use **is** when writing about one thing, but **are** for more than one.

The rabbit **is** walking in the forest. The rabbits **are** walking in the forest.

In the past tense we use **was** or **were**.

The duck **was** fat. The ducks **were** fat.

A Use **is** or **are** to complete these sentences.
1. He _____ reading a story.
2. She _____ writing a letter.
3. The boys _____ working hard.
4. It _____ time for bed.
5. The cups _____ on the tray.

B Complete these sentences using **was** or **were**.
1. The men _____ digging up the road.
2. The boy _____ watching them.
3. The waves _____ crashing on the rocks.
4. They _____ too tired to walk any farther.
5. She _____ nearly an hour late.

C Complete these sentences with **is, are, was** or **were**.
1. The tray _____ on the table when I saw it.
2. Listen! The birds _____ singing.
3. I am reading and they _____ painting until it _____ time to go out.
4. The house _____ noisy at the moment, but the grounds _____ peaceful.
5. Kate _____ up early, and made breakfast while the twins _____ still in bed.
6. Yesterday they _____ trying to finish the job while there _____ still time.

Dear Bunny …

Imagine you are the rabbit in the story of "The Rabbit and the Wolf". Write a letter to a friend saying what the wolf did to you, and warning your friend about him.

16 Burrow Close
The Forest
BUN1 3ZZ

6th June

Dear Bunny,

Thanks for your letter. By the time you receive my letter you should have finished digging that extension to your burrow. Have a rest, put your feet up and read all about my narrow escape from a wolf!

Bunny Brighteye
17 The Warren
Green Woods
BUN5 9XX

Day 5 S

Getting verbs to agree

Verbs change according to who is doing the action:

I **am** swimming.
He **is** swimming.
We **are** swimming.

A Complete these sentences with suitable words: **am, is, are, was, were.**

1. Daljit _____ playing the piano and I _____ playing the recorder.
2. I _____ painting, you _____ drawing and the others _____ making a model.
3. Yesterday when I _____ shopping, my friends _____ looking for me.
4. We _____ working, but you _____ watching TV.
5. _____ Jake coming? We _____ getting tired of waiting.
6. _____ I the captain of this team or _____ you?
7. _____ we late or _____ you early?
8. It _____ raining when Simon and Jason _____ playing football.

B Use each of these words in a sentence of your own: **am, is, are, was, were.**

Polly and the Wolf

In her "Polly and the Wolf" stories Catherine Storr matches the traditional wolf against a modern young girl. This extract tells of Polly's first meeting with the wolf.

One day Polly was alone downstairs. Camilla was using the Hoover upstairs, so when the front door bell rang, Polly went to open the door. There was a great black wolf! He put his foot inside the door and said:

"Now I'm going to eat you up!"

"Oh no, please," said Polly. "I don't want to be eaten up."

"Oh, yes," said the wolf, "I am going to eat you. But first tell me, what is that delicious smell?"

"Come down to the kitchen," said Polly, "and I will show you."

She led the wolf down to the kitchen. There on the table was a delicious-looking pie.

"Have a slice?" said Polly. The wolf's mouth watered, and he said, "Yes, please!"

Polly cut him a big piece. When he had eaten it, the wolf asked for another, and then for another.

"Now," said Polly, after the third helping, "what about me?"

"Sorry," said the wolf, "I'm too full of pie. I'll come back another day to deal with you."

A week later Polly was alone again, and again the bell rang. Polly ran to open the door. There was the wolf again.

"This time I'm really going to eat you up, Polly," said the wolf.

"All right," said Polly, "but first, just smell."

The wolf took a long breath. "Delicious!" he said. "What is it?"

"Come down and see," said Polly.

In the kitchen was a large chocolate cake.

"Have a slice?" said Polly.

"Yes," said the wolf greedily. He ate six big slices.

"Now, what about me?" said Polly.

"Sorry," said the wolf, "I just haven't got room. I'll come back." He slunk out of the back door.

*from **Clever Polly and the Stupid Wolf** by Catherine Storr*

Polly tricks the wolf

A This chart tells us what happened at the beginning of the story of "Polly and the Wolf" on page 41. Copy and complete the chart by adding three sentences of your own telling what happened next.

The wolf came to eat Polly.

↓

She took him to the kitchen and gave him a big piece of pie.

↓

He was too full to eat her so he went away.

B Write a few sentences saying what happens when the wolf comes back a third time.

The apostrophe

When people speak, they use short forms of some words. The **apostrophe**, or raised comma, shows us where one or more letters have been missed out.

   I'm = I am   don't = do not   haven't = have not

A Write the short form of these words:
1. cannot
2. did not
3. I have
4. he will
5. could not
6. they are
7. you are
8. I am
9. she is
10. do not
11. I will

B Rewrite these sentences using short forms.
1. **He will** be here soon, so **do not** mess up the room or **I will** be cross.
2. **She is** certain **it is** valuable but **he is** not sure.
3. **You are** sure that you **cannot** come to the party? **She will** be disappointed.
4. **I have** finished, **he has** nearly finished, but **you have** only just started!

Singular and plural

Singular means **one**: dog, lion, car, pen, road, flower.

Plural means **more than one**: dogs, lions, cars, pens, roads, flowers.

A Most words add an **-s** after the last letter to make the plural form. Change these singular nouns to plural by adding **-s.**
1. wall
2. computer
3. book
4. clock
5. sound
6. street
7. bird
8. chair
9. bat
10. tin

B Most words ending in **-f** or **-fe** make their plural form by changing the **-f** or **-fe** to **-ves**:

   one wol**f**, two wol**ves**
   one thie**f**, three thie**ves**
   one cal**f**, two cal**ves**

Change these singular nouns to plural:
1. self
2. life
3. wife
4. knife
5. shelf
6. elf
7. loaf
8. yourself

What happened after that?

Make up a new adventure for Polly and the wolf. Make notes of your ideas.

Plan your writing like this:

Characters: Polly, the wolf

Setting: Where does your story take place?

Beginning: How does the wolf try to catch Polly?

Middle: How does Polly trick him?

End: How does the story end?

The story "Polly and the Wolf" begins with the sentence:

One day Polly was alone downstairs.

Begin your story in a similar way:

One day Polly was …

(Think where she was, or what she was doing.)

Day 5

Getting the names right

Capital letters are used for the names of people and places:

Polly   Bristol   Catherine Storr   Australia   Cardiff   Roald Dahl

A Copy these sentences, putting capital letters where necessary.
1. tom and tess live at 12 devon street in bamford.
2. next week shireen and narinder are going to manchester.
3. rowena's favourite places are london and brighton.
4. i live in london, paul lives in edinburgh and michael lives in belfast.
5. katy used to live in canada, but now she lives in bristol.

B Copy these sentences, putting capital letters, full stops, question marks and commas where necessary.
1. where are you going katy
2. my best friends are joanne mamta sophie and louise
3. did mel say sandy comes from leeds
4. sam and gina come from peterborough, don't they
5. mrs jones went to tesco for some sugar coffee biscuits and vegetables

The Birth of the Sun

This traditional tale is told by the Australian Aborigines. It is a creation myth – a traditional explanation of how the world began. The creatures in the story are Australian birds.

When the world was very young, many many moons ago, all people had to search for food and water in the dim light of the moon, for there was no sun.

Then came a time when the emu and the brolga were both sitting on their nests of eggs. They argued violently about whose young were better. The brolga, sitting on her nest, became more and more angry, and finally, she could take no more. She left her nest and ran to the nest of her rival, took one of the emu's eggs, and hurled it into the sky, where it shattered against a pile of sticks.

The yolk of the egg burst into a bright yellow flame. The sky people, for the first time, saw the beauty of the world beneath them. They talked together of this beauty, and they decided that the inhabitants below should have more light.

They decided that every night they would collect a pile of dry wood, and set it alight as soon as the morning star appeared. This worked sometimes, but if the day was cloudy, or if there was much rain, no-one could see the star, and no-one lit the fire.

So the sky people thought of another plan. They decided to ask the kookaburra for help. The kookaburra had a strong, loud call, and they asked the bird to call them every morning, so they could light the fire.

So, when the kookaburra's rollicking laughter is first heard, the fire is lit. At first this fire in the sky throws out only a little heat and light. But by noon, the heat can be intense. Later on, the fire begins to die until only a few embers remain to colour the sky.

*from **Creation Stories**, retold by Maureen Stewart*

Day 1 A bright yellow flame

Read the tale on page 44, then put these sentences into the correct order so that they tell the story.

Beginning

The brolga threw one of the emu's eggs into the sky.

The emu and the brolga argued about whose young were better.

Middle

They built a pile of wood every night.

The egg hit a pile of sticks and burst into a bright yellow flame.

When clouds hid the star, they forgot to light the fire.

When they saw the morning star, they set fire to the wood.

The sky people saw how beautiful the world was.

Ending

So when the kookaburra is first heard, the fire is lit.

They asked the kookaburra to call them every morning.

Day 2 Describing things

Adjectives describe nouns:
a **bright** star, a **tall** man.

A Copy the headings. Sort the adjectives into those which describe colour, shape, size and mood.

Colour	Shape	Size	Mood
yellow	round	enormous	angry
square	silvery	large	green
sad	gold	excited	bent
tiny	thick	cheerful	curved

B Sort these adjectives, and add them to your lists.

red	happy	tall	white
oval	small	bored	pointed
disappointed	circular	blue	huge

C Choose three adjectives from each heading and use them in sentences of your own.

Write your own creation myth

Write your own creation myth about the sun.
Choose **one** of the following ideas.

● Write about the sky people in "The Birth of the Sun" story, but change the setting.

● Keep the setting of the story, but make up new supernatural characters.

● Make up a new explanation for how the sun was born.

● Explain why the sun rises in the morning, moves across the sky and sets in the evening.

● Explain why some days the sun hides behind the clouds.

Plan your story with a beginning, middle and ending.

Begin your story:
When the world was very young ...

More about adjectives

A Copy and complete these sentences with suitable adjectives from the list.

smooth	sunny	tasty
easy	round	rainy
untidy	big	

1. The food was _____.
2. Mum was cross because his room was very _____.
3. We had _____ weather on Saturday, but it was _____ on Sunday.
4. The pebble was _____ and very _____.
5. The box was _____ but _____ to lift.

B Copy and complete these sentences with suitable adjectives of your own.
1. The _____ car was _____ and _____.
2. They had a _____ meal at a _____ cafe at the end of a _____ lane.
3. We had a _____ time at the seaside. The sea was _____ and the beach _____.
4. The _____ garden had a _____ path leading to a _____ tree.
5. We had a _____ picnic in a _____ spot by a _____ stream.

Opposites

The opposite of **weak** is **strong**.

A Find opposites for these adjectives.
1. dark
2. fat
3. quick
4. high
5. rough
6. rich
7. tall
8. heavy

B Use each of the opposites you have found in a sentence of your own.

Instructions

Chocolate Coconut Balls

This is a simple recipe for a Hindu sweet which is often made at Diwali time.

Ingredients
225g desiccated coconut
100g icing sugar
1 small can condensed milk (200g)
250g block of cooking chocolate, for coating
Waxed paper on which to set finished sweets (paper from a cornflakes packet is ideal)

Method
1. Mix coconut and sugar with the milk. If coconut is very dry, use less than the quantity given, or sweets may go hard.
2. Make small balls from the mixture.
3. Melt chocolate in a small basin over a pan of simmering water.
4. To coat the balls, drop them into the melted chocolate, lift each one out with a fork and tap it on the edge of the bowl to allow excess chocolate to drop off.
5. Put balls on waxed paper to set.

from **Divali** *by Howard Marsh*

Vanishing Colours

White light is made up of all the colours of the rainbow. This disc will make those colours change back into white or pale grey.

You will need: card, protractor, crayons, a piece of wooden rod about 15 cm long

1. Cut out a disc from the card.
2. Divide it into six equal parts, using a protractor. Each segment should have an angle of 60 degrees.
3. Colour the segments in the order colours appear in a rainbow: red, orange, yellow, green, blue and violet.
4. Make a hole in the centre of the disc and carefully push the wooden rod through so that it is fairly tight.
5. Hold the rod between your hands with the colours facing up. Rub your hands back and forth to spin the disc and watch what happens.

Make a flow chart

Read the recipe on page 47, then copy and complete this flow chart showing how to make chocolate coconut balls.

1. Mix coconut and sugar with the milk. If coconut is very dry, use less than the quantity given, or sweets may go hard.

↓

2.

↓

3.

↓

4.

↓

5.

Making notes

The key words in this instruction have been **emphasised**:

> **Mix coconut** and **sugar** with the **milk.** **If coconut** is **very dry, use less** than the quantity given, **or sweets may go hard**.

The key words may then be written as notes:

> Mix coconut, sugar, milk. If coconut very dry, use less or sweets may go hard.

Pick out the key words in the recipe for chocolate coconut balls. Write them as notes.

Verbs in the first, second and third person

Verbs may be in the first person (I or we): **I am** mixing the ingredients.

Or the second person (you): **Mix** the ingredients.

Or the third person (he, she, it or they): **He is** mixing the ingredients. **They are** mixing the ingredients.

A Change these third person verbs to the second person. The first one has been done for you.
1. She cuts out a disc from the card.
   Cut out a disc from the card.
2. They go down the corridor.
3. He divides it into six equal parts.
4. She takes the first turn left.
5. He mixes flour and water into a paste.

B Change these second person verbs to the third person. The first one has been done for you.
1. Make a hole in the centre of the disc.
   She makes a hole in the centre of the disc.
2. Plant the seeds 5 cm apart.
3. Mix all the ingredients together.
4. Insert the disc into the computer.
5. Go to the shops and buy some sugar.

C Change these third person verbs to the first person. The first one has been done for you.
1. They went to town.
   We **went** to town.
2. He is going to the shops.
3. She reads a book.
4. He swims every Friday.
5. They are playing chess tonight.

D Which person are these verbs? Write first, second or third. The first one has been done for you.
1. I took a wrong turn.
   First
2. Go away.
3. We went away.
4. Stop!
5. She cut two slices of bread.
6. Butter each slice.
7. We ate the sandwiches.

Write your own instructions

Write your own instructions for doing one of these things.

● Write about the sky people in "The Birth of the Sun" story, but change the setting.

● How to make a cup of tea

● How to record a TV programme

● How to make a sandwich

● How to use the telephone

● How to load a computer program

1. Put water in the kettle and switch on.
2. Put tea in the teapot.
3.

Number each stage. When you have finished, check that you have not missed anything out, and that everything is in the right order.

Write a recipe

1. Write a recipe for one of your favourite dishes. Use these headings to help you:
Ingredients   Equipment   Method
2. Make up a magic recipe with horrible ingredients. Use headings for your recipe.

Word building

A Match these words so that they make a new word. The first one has been done for you.

tea — light
gold   brush
book — pot
news   house
water   case
grape   mat
head   paper
door   fruit
green   fish
hair   fall

Some short words can be joined together to make a longer word:

rain + bow = rainbow
class + room = classroom

B Use each new word in a sentence of your own.

Games

Achi

Achi is a game for two players played by children in Ghana.

Equipment:
a board as shown
4 counters each

Rules:
1 The aim of this game is to get three counters in a line. The players take turns to place one of their counters on an empty point where lines join.
2 When all eight counters have been placed, each player may move along a line to an empty point.
3 The winner is the first player to get three counters in a row, down, across or diagonally.

Nine Men's Morris

This is a very old game for two players.

Equipment:
a board as shown
9 counters each

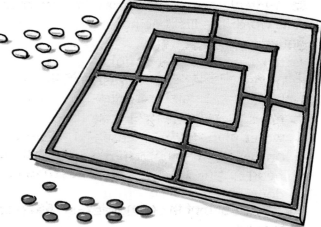

Rules:
Each player has nine "men" or counters. Taking turns, each player puts one counter on one of the points on the board where two lines join. The aim of the game is to get three counters in a row. Once a player has done this, he or she is allowed to remove one of the opponent's men from the board.
Once all the pieces are on the board, the players take turns in moving a man from one point to an empty point which is next door to it and joined directly by a line. Each time a player gets three men in a row, he or she may remove one of the other player's men. The winner is the player who leaves an opponent with just two men or when the opponent is blocked and unable to move.

How to play

Look at the games described on page 50, then answer these questions for each game.

A

1. How many people can play?
2. What equipment is needed?
3. How is the game won?

B

1. In what ways are these games similar?
2. How is Achi similar to noughts and crosses?
3. A morris is a kind of dance. Explain why Nine Men's Morris is so called.

Confusing words: to, too, two

He is going **to** the park.

The box is **too** heavy.

This is a game for **two** players.

A Copy and complete these sentences with **to**, **too** or **two**.

1. The work was _____ hard.
2. We are going _____ school.
3. The road was _____ busy to cross safely.
4. It is _____ minutes _____ seven.
5. The _____ girls were going _____ the shops.
6. The next train _____ London leaves at _____ o'clock.

B Write a sentence of your own for each word: **to, too, two.**

Missing letters

A These words have missing letters.
Copy and complete each word.

1. w _ _ n _ r: the person who wins
2. b _ _ r d: a playing surface for a game
3. d _ _ e: small cubes with numbers on, used in games
4. _ _ rd _ : you need a pack of these to play Snap

B Use each of the completed words in a sentence of your own.

Pairing up

A Some words go together in pairs:

snakes and ladders,
knife and fork.

Match up these words into word pairs:

bat	pins	salt
night	ball	bucket
mustard	lock	saucer
cress	spade	day
needles	key	pepper
cup		

B Choose three of the word pairs and use them in sentences of your own.

Rules for a board game

Choose a board game you know well.
Write your own instructions for playing it.

Use these headings in your instructions:

Number of players

Equipment

Aim

Rules

Word fun

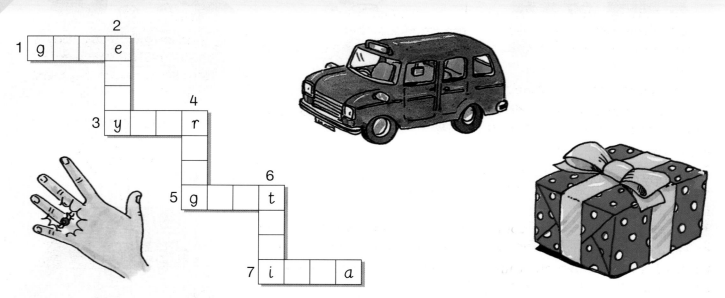

A Use the clues to complete the word steps above.
1. a sticky liquid for joining things together
2. not difficult
3. twelve months
4. jewellery worn on the finger
5. something given as a present
6. a car people pay to ride in
7. a sudden thought of a way of doing something

B Unscramble these colour words.
1. der
2. elub
3. glod
4. thiew
5. knip
6. pleurp
7. visler
8. agrone
9. igindo
10. nowbr

C Add a letter to these words to make a new word. The first one has been done for you.
1. <u>b</u>one
2. _own
3. _eel
4. car_
5. _lace
6. _link
7. than_
8. shin_
9. hop_
10. _top
11. rust_
12. _cream
13. pain_
14. _lean
15. was_
16. _right

D Choose four of the words you made and use them in sentences of your own.

The Meaning of Words

A dictionary and a thesaurus are two very useful word books.
A dictionary is an alphabetical list of words and their meanings.
A thesaurus is a book in which words with similar meanings
(synonyms) are grouped together.

Dictionary

Nn

nail
1   A nail is a small piece of metal with a point on one end. It usually
   has a flat top that you can hit with a hammer. Nails are
   sometimes used to join two pieces of wood together.
2   Your nails are the thin hard areas that cover the end of each of
   your fingers and toes.

name   A name is what somebody or something is called.

narrow (narrower, narrowest) Something that is narrow is a very
short distance from one side to the other.

nasty (nastier, nastiest)
1   Someone who is nasty is very unkind.
2   Something that is nasty is very unpleasant.

native
1   A native of a particular country is someone who was born there.
2   Your native country is the country where you were born.

natural is used to describe things that are not made by people. Trees,
rocks and rivers are natural things.

nature is everything in the world that is not caused by human beings.

naughty (naughtier, naughtiest) A child who is naughty behaves
badly.

navigate Someone who navigates a ship or aircraft works out which
way to go.

navy
1   A navy is one of the forces that a country uses for fighting.
   Navies use ships to fight at sea.
2   Navy blue is a very dark blue colour.

near (nearer, nearest)
1   If you are near to something, you are only a short distance from it.
2   If something happens near to a particular point in time, it happens
   close to it: *It happens somewhere near the beginning of the story.*

from **Collins Primary Dictionary**

Thesaurus

gentle
placid
easygoing
mild

**This *gentle* horse is the best
one for you to ride.**

silent
quiet as a mouse

**Be *silent* or you'll frighten
the squirrel away.**

restful

**Mum and Dad say they
need a *restful* weekend at
home after working hard
all week.**

still
peaceful
calm
hushed
tranquil

**The forest is *still* at night,
far away from the noisy city.**

quiet sounds

hiss	swish
hum	tick
murmur	tinkle
rustle	whisper
sigh	

from **Collins Junior
Thesaurus**

Day 1 Looking up words

Look at the extracts on page 53, then answer these questions.

A

1. Write out three words from the dictionary which have more than one meaning,
2. What does "navigate" mean?
3. Write out four synonyms for "still" that you have found in the thesaurus.
4. Choose a word for a quiet sound, and use it in a sentence of your own.

B

1. Explain why a dictionary is a useful book.
2. How is a thesaurus useful?
3. Use these words in sentences of your own: swish, timid, peaceful.

 W

Day 2 Alphabetical order

a b c d e f g h i j k l m n o p q r s t u v w x y z

The words in a dictionary are listed in alphabetical order to help us find them easily.

ape, bear, cat, snake, zebra

When two words begin with the same letter, the second letter is used for alphabetical order:

deer, dinosaur, donkey, dragon, duck

A Rewrite these lists in the order you would find them in a dictionary.
1. time, two, tree, three, took
2. some, sister, school, saw, should

B Do the same with these.
1. but, brother, because, boy, by
2. what, water, would, with, were
3. load, lunch, light, large, letter
4. ceiling, cycle, catch, chimney, crisp

Synonyms

A **synonym** is a word which means the same or nearly the same as another word. These are all synonyms for **bad**:

rotten   naughty   wicked   nasty

A Find more synonyms for these words:

| **good** | **big** | **small** |
| kind | large | microscopic |

B Choose a better word from the words below for each numbered sentence.

atlas dictionary diary manual encyclopedia thesaurus

1. I looked up the meaning of the word in a **book**.
2. He bought a car repair **book**.
3. This is a **book** with lists of synonyms.
4. The **book** had maps in it.
5. There are facts on almost every subject in this **book**.
6. I keep a **book** in which I write what happens each day.

Using a dictionary

1. Take a dictionary and open it in the middle. Which letter do the words begin with? ___
2. Now open it a quarter way through. Which letter do those words begin with? ___
3. Do the same at the three quarters mark. Which letter now? ___

Words beginning with the letters A to D take up roughly the first quarter.

Words beginning with the letters E to L take up roughly the second quarter.

Words beginning M to R take up roughly the third quarter.

Words beginning S to Z take up roughly the last quarter.

4. Each box represents a quarter of the dictionary. For each one write the starting letters you would expect to find there. The first one has been done for you.

1st	2nd	3rd	4th
ABCD			

5. In which quarter would you would expect to find these words? Write 1st, 2nd, 3rd or 4th for each one. Do it like this: *a)* 1st

a) cap   b) sit   c) pet   d) wise   e) dog
f) net   g) tree   h) ball   i) holly   j) mess
k) rust   l) drag   m) quiet   n) ice   o) gate
p) eel   q) yacht   r) kettle   s) open   t) job

Finding out

Use a dictionary to find the answers to these questions. See how quickly you can find each word.
1. What is a **jungle**?
2. What does **gradual** mean?
3. What is a **sultana**?
4. What is a **hexagon**?
5. What does **famous** mean?
6. What is a **satellite**?
7. Is a **limpet** a bird?

Definitions

The definition of a word is its meaning. Write your own definition for these words. Check your work with a dictionary when you have finished.

1. child	5. plank	9. cup
2. key	6. skin	10. tale
3. litter	7. mask	
4. hat	8. kitten	

Silent letters

The letters in some words are silent:

g(h)ost, (k)nee, com(b), (w)rite

A Copy down these words, and then draw a ring round the silent letters:

1. could	5. whisper	9. who	13. knock
2. know	6. calm	10. climb	14. wrong
3. what	7. rustle	11. should	15. lamb
4. should	8. would	12. night	16. two

B Choose ten words with silent letters and use them in sentences of your own.

Rats!

This is the beginning of a very well-known traditional story, The Pied Piper of Hamelin.

Once upon a time, and this was a long time ago, the people of Hamelin were not very happy. And they had good reason. Their town was overrun with rats. They were everywhere, hundreds and thousands of them, and the numbers were growing by the day.

Wherever the people turned there were rats: scuttling in the cellars, scampering on the roofs, sliding through the windows. They even climbed down the chimneys. The found their way into every barn, every store-room, every house and every cupboard. What were they after? Food, of course.

Oh, they were greedy rats. They ate all the corn which was stored for the winter. They ate the cheese as fast as it was made. The fruit was no sooner picked that it was gobbled up by the rats.

They drank the milk from the buckets. They supped the wine and all the beer in the barrels. Soon there was little food or drink left for the people of the town. The place was hardly worth living in.

As the people got thinner, the rats grew fatter and this made them even bolder. Now they weren't afraid of being chased away, they were up to all kinds of mischief.

from **The Pied Piper of Hamelin** *by Rose Impey*

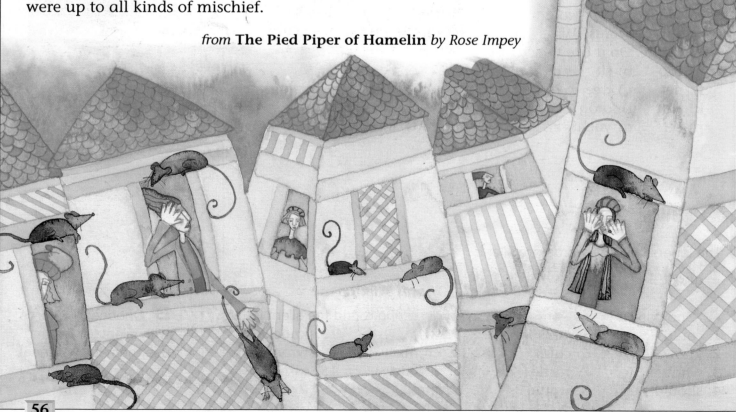

Make a storyboard

This is the first picture in a storyboard of the Pied Piper story. It shows what happens in the first paragraph of the extract on page 56. Continue the story by drawing a picture and writing a caption for each of the remaining four paragraphs.

Headlines

The headlines in a newspaper give the main idea of a news report in just a few words.

Notice that only the most important words have been used in the headlines.

Make up a headline of your own for each of these reports. Use the key words to help you. We have **emphasised** the key words in the first sentence to get you started.

a) The **rats** are **eating all** the **food** in **Hamelin**.
b) Hamelin is a place not worth living in.
c) As the people get thinner, the rats grow fatter.
d) The Hamelin rats get bolder.
e) The rats get up to all kinds of mischief.

Reading for clues

We can often guess the meaning of a new word by thinking about the sense of the whole sentence. Read this sentence:

The people of Hamelin were horrified because their food stocks were eaten by **vermin**.

We can guess that **vermin** are living creatures which destroy food.

A full definition of vermin is: small animals or insects, such as rats or cockroaches, which carry disease and damage crops or food.

A Read these sentences. Make your own guess at the meaning of the **emphasised** words. Then use a dictionary to see how close you were to a full definition.

1. The water we drink is first stored in a **reservoir**.
2. Many people died from lack of food during the **famine**.
3. The farmer cut the corn by driving the **combine harvester** through the cornfield.
4. The **supersonic** plane flew faster than the speed of sound.
5. The **typhoon** blew roofs off the houses.

B Work out the meaning of these words:
1. He spilled some of his coffee because the cup was filled to the **brim**.
2. Fruit contains **vitamins** to keep you healthy.
3. The **navigator** worked out the best way to get to the island.
4. During the **eclipse** the moon covered most of the sun.
5. Iceland has a cold **climate**, but India is hot.

C Use each of these words in a sentence of your own to show its meaning.
1. cupboard 4. greedy
2. mischief 5. worth
3. cellar 6. scamper

A new Pied Piper story

Imagine that your school is overun by cats, mice, wasps or some other creature. Write a new Pied Piper story telling what happens when he comes to help you.

Write your story like this:

Getting started
Where is your story set? What kind of creature becomes a nuisance?

Planning
Paragraph 1: What happens when the creatures overrun your school?

Paragraph 2: What happens when you ask the Pied Piper to help?

Paragraph 3: How does your story end?

Checking your work
Have you missed anything out?

Is everything in the right order?

Is your ending interesting?

Underline any words you aren't sure of. Check these with a dictionary or word bank.

Circle letters which should be capitals. Add any missing full stops, commas, question marks or exclamation marks.

Final draft
Copy out your work in your best writing, or use a word processor. Include all your changes and corrections.

Keep in step

A Use the clues to complete this opposites word step.
Each answer is the **opposite** of the word given.
1. hot
2. light
3. cruel
4. cheap
5. imaginary
6. early
7. west

B Find opposites for these words:

low   laugh   tight   dull   wet
slow   last   new   long   quiet

C Use each of the opposites from exercise B in a sentence of your own.

58

Odysseus and Polyphemus

Odysseus is a famous hero in the myths of Ancient Greece. A myth is a story which is not based on historical fact and often features gods, goddesses and fantastic creatures. This story tells what happens when Odysseus and his crew take shelter in the cave of the Cyclops, Polyphemus.

The Cyclopes were giants. Each had only one enormous eye in the middle of his forehead. They lived in wild, faraway places where there were no laws. Each Cyclops lived alone, tending his sheep and goats. One was named Polyphemus, and he was the son of Poseidon, god of the sea.

Long ago a man named Odysseus was sailing home from war. He and his crew went ashore on Polyphemus' island, where they made themselves comfortable in the giant's cave.

When Polyphemus returned that evening with his flocks, he was furious to see strangers in his home. He closed the entrance to the cave with a gigantic rock only he was strong enough to move. Then he killed and ate some of the unlucky sailors.

Odysseus didn't try to take revenge that night, but while Polyphemus slept he stayed awake, waiting. When he heard the giant snoring loudly, he poked a red-hot stick into his one enormous eye and blinded him.

In the morning Odysseus and his remaining crew clung to the woolly bellies of the giant's rams. The animals left the cave as Polyphemus counted them one by one by patting their backs. The blinded Polyphemus couldn't see that Odysseus and the sailors were safely hidden beneath his long-haired beasts.

Odysseus paid a high price for his cleverness. He hadn't known that Polyphemus was the son of Poseidon, and now the god of the sea was angry with him. He punished Odysseus by making it impossible for him to return to his home on the small, rocky island of Ithaca.

from **The One-eyed Giant and Other Monsters from the Greek Myths** *by Anne Rockwell*

Caught by a giant!

A Read the extract on page 59, then answer these questions in complete sentences.
1. What was unusual about the Cyclopes?
2. Where did they live?
3. Who was the father of Polyphemus?
4. Where did Odysseus and his men stay the night?
5. What did Polyphemus do when he found them there?

B Do the same with these questions.
1. Why do you think Odysseus blinded Polyphemus?
2. How did Odysseus and his men escape?
3. How did Poseidon punish Odysseus?

More suffixes

Words ending in **y** change the **y** to **i** before adding **-ness** or **-ful**: happiness, beautiful

As we learned in Unit 11, a suffix is a letter or letters added to the end of a word to change its meaning.

The suffix -**ness** changes some adjectives into nouns: clever + ness = cleverness

The suffix -**ful** changes some nouns into adjectives: wonder + ful = wonderful.

The suffix -**less** means "without something": pain + less = painless (without pain)

A Make new words by adding **-ness** or **-ful** to these words.
1. happy
2. care
3. hard
4. help
5. bright
6. beauty
7. tidy
8. lazy

B Make new words from these by adding **-less**. Use each word in a sentence.
1. care
2. fear
3. use
4. hope
5. colour
6. roof

More plurals

Many words ending in **y** make their plurals by changing the **y** to **ies**:

cherry	cherries
spy	spies
lorry	lorries

A few words do not change at all when making the plural form:

sheep	deer	cod
salmon	trout	vermin

A Make these words plural:
1. penny
2. fly
3. sky
4. ferry
5. body
6. try
7. curry
8. bully
9. story
10. berry

B Choose three of the plurals you have made. Use each one in a sentence.

C Change these words to plural. Then choose three plurals and use each of them in a sentence.
1. reply
2. ruby
3. baby
4. butterfly
5. party
6. lady
7. pony
8. cry
9. family
10. cherry

Further adventures of Odysseus and Polyphemus

Write a sequel to the story of Odysseus and Polyphemus.
Imagine a storm drives Odysseus and the sailors back to the
island where Polyphemus is waiting to take his revenge.

Plan your story like this:

Paragraph 1: the beginning
Odysseus takes shelter from a storm on the island.

Blind Polyphemus hears them approaching.

He recognises the voice of Odysseus.

How does this make him feel?

Paragraph 2: the middle
Polyphemus decides to set a trap.

How does he catch them?

How does he feel now?

What does he plan to do with the sailors?

Paragraph 3: the ending
How do Odysseus and his men escape this time?

Collective nouns

Collective nouns stand for a group of
people, animals or things.

a **crew** of sailors   a **flock** of sheep
a **bunch** of grapes

A Find group names for these:
1. a _____ of cattle
2. a _____ of bees
3. a _____ of wolves
4. a _____ of birds
5. an _____ of soldiers
6. a _____ of players

B Complete these phrases:
1. a pride of _____
2. a gaggle of _____
3. a school of _____
4. a litter of _____
5. a bouquet of _____
6. a fleet of _____

C Choose three
collective nouns from
exercise A and three
from exercise B. Use
each one in a
sentence of your own.

The Spell-Hound

The hero of this tale is Erik, a Viking warrior who lived hundreds and hundreds of years ago. He has set out on a dangerous voyage to find the land where the sun goes at night.

Scarcely had the ship left the bay, however, than Thorkhild gave a cry, and they all turned and saw a great black dog standing at the helm of the ship.

"Look at its eyes!" cried Thorkhild, and they all saw that in its glowing yellow eyes, it had no pupils.

"Is it blind?" asked Erik, but no one could tell, and the dog neither barked nor moved. It merely stood there at the helm, and the tiller seemed to move of its own accord.

"This is no mortal dog," said Thorkhild, "this is a spell-hound!" And there was not one amongst them that dared go near the helm, as long as that black dog stood there.

The wind blew and the *Golden Dragon* sped through the seas, with the black dog at the tiller until at last Thorkhild turned to Erik and said: "I have heard my grandfather tell of such a dog boarding ships in the far long ago. Sometimes it would steer a ship to an island, where they found unimaginable treasure. But sometimes it would steer a ship over the edge of the world."

"How can we tell which way this spell-hound will steer us?" asked Ragnar Forkbeard.

"That I do not know," replied Thorkhild.

Erik was silent for a while, and *Golden Dragon* sped on through the salt spray, while the black dog stood, unmoving, by the tiller. And Erik's men whispered one to the other, "We are heading for the edge of the world!"

from **The Saga of Erik the Viking** *by Terry Jones*

Aboard a Viking ship

Read the extract on page 62, then answer these questions in complete sentences.

A
1. What was the name of the ship?
2. Where was the spell-hound standing?
3. Who knew about the spell-hound?
4. Where did the ship's crew think they were heading?

B
1. Describe the spell-hound.
2. Why was it important to know which way the spell-hound would steer the ship?

Using a thesaurus

Suppose we wanted a synonym for **glowing** in this sentence:

> The spell-hound had **glowing** yellow eyes with no pupils.

A glow is a kind of light. If we look up "glow" in a thesaurus index it points us to synonyms for "light". **Collins Junior Thesaurus** gives this list of synonyms for what lights do:

burn	glint
flare	glisten
flash	glitter
flicker	glow
glare	shimmer
gleam	sparkle
glimmer	twinkle

A Make your own list of suitable words to replace **glowing** in the sentence about the spell-hound's eyes.

B Choose a word from the list above to replace **burned** or **burning** in the sentences below.
1. Light **burned** from the lighthouse.
2. The stars **burned** in the night sky.
3. The snow **burned** in the moonlight.
4. The fire cast a **burning** light over the room.
5. The jewel **burned** in the sunlight.

C Use a thesaurus to find suitable words to replace the **emphasised** word in each of these sentences:
1. There was a short **stop** before the concert began.
2. It was **cold** when the heating broke down.
3. Take care not to **fall** on the stairs.
4. The fence had a **break** in it.
5. I **like** cats.
6. The sea was very **rough**.

D Use these synonyms in sentences of your own: guess, expect, believe, imagine.

Describe the spell-hound

A Imagine you were a member of Erik the Viking's crew when the spell-hound appeared. Write a letter telling a friend about the spell-hound, what it looked like, how it behaved and what happened to you.

16 Sea View,
Seaport,
Lincs
OCE AN3

2nd April

Dear Sam,

I've just returned from a most amazing voyage, and I'm lucky to be alive!

B Design a poster warning sailors about the spell-hound.
a) Make up an eye-catching heading.
b) Draw a picture of the spell-hound.
c) Explain how it behaves, and why it is dangerous.
d) Give advice on how to deal with it.

Finding the right word

A Copy and complete these sentences, using the correct word from the ones in brackets.
1. Erik (was/were) silent for a while.
2. We (am/is/are) heading for the edge of the world.
3. There (is/are) five minutes left.
4. My friend and I (am/is/are) going to the party.
5. She (see/saw) her cousin yesterday.
6. The sun (rise/rises) in the east.

B Copy and complete these sentences, using the correct word from the ones in brackets.
1. One of the children (was/were) injured.
2. He (hurt/hurted) his arm.
3. I (saw/seen) her score a goal.
4. He (bring/brings) me a newspaper every day.
5. They (write/writes) a letter every week.
6. He (speak/speaks) very loudly.
7. The children (sing/sings) beautifully.
8. The cups (was/were) broken, but a saucer (was/were) undamaged.

C Use each of these words in a sentence of your own:

do, does, go, goes, swim, swims

Alphabetic Lists

Index

B
Black
panthers 5, 16, 20, 21

C
Cheetahs 5, 6, 18–19, 25
Claws 4
Cubs 10, 24–5

F
Food 4, 9, 11, 12, 14, 19, 22, 23, 24
Fur 12, 14, 16, 18, 26

H
Hunting 4, 8, 11, 14, 19, 20, 22–3, 24, 27, 28

J
Jaguars 5, 6, 18, 22, 23

L
Leopards 4, 6, 14–15, 23
Lions 4, 6, 8–9, 10–11, 14, 23

M
Manes 8
Markings 14, 16, 18, 20

P
Paws 23
Prides 10, 11
Pumas 4, 6, 16–17, 26

R
Roaring 11

S
Siberian tigers 6, 12
Snow leopards 6, 14, 20

T
Tails 14
Teeth 4
Tigers 5, 6, 12–13, 14, 20, 21, 23, 28

from **Let's Look at Big Cats** *by Rhoda Nottridge*

Using an index

Scan the index on page 65 for the following subjects. Write down the page numbers.

1. markings
2. snow leopards
3. claws
4. fur
5. jaguars
6. teeth
7. prides
8. roaring
9. cubs
10. Siberian tigers

When two words begin with the same letter, the second letter is used for alphabetical order.

Rewrite this list in alphabetical order.

gorilla alligator lynx antelope elephant
camel penguin jaguar aardvark giraffe
llama panda

Using a dictionary

You will need a dictionary to help you answer these questions.

A Complete these words for the pictures at the bottom of the page:

1. br _ _ c h
2. p _ r _ _ l
3. j_w_l _ _ ry
4. phe_s_ nt
5. d i _ _ _ _ d
6. r _ d _ _ _ o _
7. t _ _ b _ _ r _ n _
8. f _ _ n _ _ _ n

B Think for yourself what the **emphasised** word means in each of the following sentences. Write down your guess and then check the meaning in a dictionary.

1. **Locusts** fly together in great numbers and often cause great damage by eating crops.
   I think a locust is ...
   The dictionary definition is ...
2. The teacher wrote the **symbol** for plus on the blackboard.
3. A kangaroo is a **marsupial** because it carries its babies in a pouch at the front.
4. The clock ticked as its **pendulum** swung to and fro.

C Find these words in your dictionary. Write sentences of your own to show two possible meanings for each of them.

1. post
2. crane
3. wave
4. rule
5. straw

D Find these words in your dictionary. Write sentences of your own to show two possible meanings for each of them.

1. ring
2. marble
3. cross
4. fly
5. plug
6. present

1.   2.   3.   4.   5.   7.   6.   8.

Alphabetically ordered texts

Use the ideas on this page to make your own alphabetic texts.

An alphabetic list
Make an alphabetic list of sports or pop personalities, or other celebrities. Remember that lists of names are in alphabetical order of **surname** (family name).

A telephone directory
Make a telephone directory of your friends and relatives.

An animal dictionary
Make an animal dictionary. Use reference books to help you write a few sentences about each animal. Add pictures to make this an illustrated dictionary.

An information book
Make a book which presents information in alphabetical order, such as a book on fruit with a page each for apples, bananas, etc. When you have finished, make an index with page references. Other subjects you might choose are: drinks, vegetables, sports, types of car, or a subject of your choice.

A glossary
Make a glossary of words linked to a current class topic, your own hobby, special interest, or another subject.

Working with information books

You will need information books on animals to answer these questions.

1. Write down the titles of books which give information on these animals.
   a) frogs
   b) crocodiles
   c) elephants
2. Scan the index in each book. Write down the page numbers where you might find out about these subjects:
   Frogs: **a)** tadpoles **b)** food **c)** skin
   Crocodiles: **a)** teeth **b)** habitat **c)** food
   Elephants: **a)** young **b)** trunk **c)** tusks
3. Use the index in a book about elephants to help you find the differences between an **Indian** and an **African** elephant.

Unit 22

Word Play

Rules

Do not jump on ancient uncles.
Do not yell at average mice.
Do not wear a broom to breakfast.
Do not take a snake's advice.
Do not bathe in chocolate pudding.
Do not talk to bearded bears.
Do not smoke cigars on sofas.
Do not dance on velvet chairs.
Do not take a whale to visit
Russell's mother's cousin's yacht.
And whatever else you do do
It is better you
Do not.

Karla Kuskin

Whipper-snapper

Whipper-snapper, rooty-tooty,
Helter-skelter, tutti-frutti;
Have a wing-ding, silly Billy,
Lickety-split, don't shally-shilly,
Niminy-piminy, willy-nilly,
Hocus-pocus, there's a dear.
Hippety-hoppety, hurry-scurry,
Mumbo-jumbo, don't you worry;
Hurdy-gurdy plays by ear.
Pop's a jim-jam fuddy-duddy,
Namby-pamby is dear muddy;
Pop's a hunky-dory foola,
Muddy, she does hula-hula …
Be an eager-beaver, Beulah.

Willard R. Espy

Recipe for a Hippopotamus Sandwich

A hippo sandwich is easy to make.
All you do is simply take
One slice of bread,
One slice of cake,
Some mayonnaise,
One onion ring,
One hippopotamus,
One piece of string,
A dash of pepper –
That ought to do it.
And now comes the problem …
Biting into it!

Shel Silverstein

Teacher said …

You can use
    mumbled and muttered,
    groaned, grumbled and uttered
    professed, droned or stuttered
        … but don't use SAID!

You can use
    rant or recite
    yell, yodel or snort
    bellow, murmur or moan
    you can use grunt or just groan
        … but don't use SAID!

You can use
    hum, howl and hail
    scream, screech, shriek or bawl
    squeak, snivel or squeal
    with a blood-curdling wail
        … but don't use SAID!
        … SAID my teacher.

Judith Nicholls

Get your teeth into a hippo!

Read the poems on page 68, then answer these questions in complete sentences.

A
1. What ingredients do you need to make a hippopotamus sandwich?
2. Which line do you like best in "Rules"? Why?
3. Read "Whipper-snapper". Write five double words you like the sound of.
4. What is amusing about the last line in "Teacher said …"?

B
1. Which poem do you like best? Why?
2. Draw a picture about your favourite poem.

More synonyms

In her poem "Teacher said …" Judith Nicholls uses many words which are synonyms of **said**:

groaned, grumbled, mumbled, screamed, moaned, bellowed

A Choose a suitable word from the list above to complete each of these sentences:
1. "Get off that wall!" he _____.
2. "Oh no, not you again!" _____ the park keeper.
3. We could not tell what she said because she _____.
4. "Aargh!" _____ the girl.
5. "I'm hurt," _____ the girl.
6. "It's not fair," he _____. "They never pick me to play."

B Write your own sentences to show the meaning of each of these words.
1. complained
2. yelled
3. whispered
4. exclaimed
5. promised

C Find four synonyms for **laugh** and use them in sentences of your own.

Rhymes

Words rhyme when they have the same sound:
bears and **chairs.**

A Find four rhyming words for each of these.
1. ring
2. shell
3. mice
4. dear
5. light
6. dark
7. cake

B Find four rhyming words for **bee** and use each one in a sentence.

Using poems as patterns

The poems in this unit may be used as patterns for new ones. Choose one or more of the ideas below for a poem of your own.

- Use "Teacher said ..." as a pattern for your own poem using synonyms. Here is an idea for the first verse to start you off.

  Teacher said ...
  You can use
  > left, departed, set off,
  > travelled and journeyed,
  > vanished, disappeared or escaped
  > > ... but don't use WENT!

  For verses 2, 3 and 4 think of synonyms for **walked**, **ran** and **moved**.

- Write your own poem using the same pattern as "Rules".

- Make a collection of double words for a new verse for the poem "Whipper-snapper". Here are some to start you off:

  pell-mell, knick-knack, dilly-dally, humdrum, wishy-washy, higgledy-piggledy

- Write a new recipe using "Recipe for a Hippopotamus Sandwich" as a pattern. What is your main ingredient: an elephant? a rhinocerous? a crocodile? or something else? Make a list of your other ingredients.

- The poem "On the Ning Nang Nong" uses sound to create effect. Write a similar poem of your own. First find a suitable title, maybe "In the Jungle Jangle Jingle" or "On the Bosh Boom Bang". Then make a list of the animals and the unusual sounds they might make.

On the Ning Nang Nong

On the Ning Nang Nong
Where the cows go Bong!
And the monkeys all say Boo!
There's a Nong Nang Ning
Where the trees go Ping!
And the tea-pots Jibber Jabber Joo.
On the Nong Ning Nang
All the mice go Clang!
And you just can't catch them when they do!
So it's Ning Nang Nong!
Cows go Bong!
Nong Nang Ning!
Trees go Ping!
Nong Ning Nang!
The mice go Clang!
What a noisy place to belong,
Is the Ning Nang Ning Nang Nong!

Spike Milligan

Alliteration

Alliteration is when several words begin with the same sound:

don't **d**illy-**d**ally

Make up alliterative lines about animals. Here are two to start you off:

Avoid angry alligators absolutely.

Busy bears build bungalows.

Day 5

More prefixes

non- means not; **mis-** means wrong:

non + sense = nonsense
mis + understand = misunderstand

anti- means against, or opposite to;
co- means together:

anti + clockwise = anticlockwise
co + operative = cooperative

A Make new words by adding **non-** or **mis-** to these words.

1. stop
2. behave
3. take
4. fiction
5. spell
6. stick
7. lay
8. fortune

B Use each of the words you made in exercise A in a sentence of your own.

C Make new words by adding **co-** or **anti-** to these words.

1. freeze
2. septic
3. biotic
4. operate
5. incidence

D Choose three of the new words you made in exercise C, and use each one in a sentence of your own.

Hiding in the Dark

It is well past midnight. Danny is very worried because his father has gone poaching and has not returned home. He decides to take a small car his father is repairing and go to look for him. Then he sees a police car coming towards him.

I didn't dare look round to see if they were stopping and coming back after me. I was certain they would stop. Any policeman in the world would stop if he suddenly passed a small boy in a tiny car chugging along a lonely road at half past two in the morning. My only thought was to get away, to escape, to vanish, though heavens knows how I was going to do that. I pressed my foot harder still on the accelerator. Then all at once I saw in my own dim headlamps the tiny gap in the hedge on my left-hand side. There wasn't time to brake or slow down, so I just yanked the wheel hard over and prayed. The little car swerved violently off the road, leaped through the gap, hit the rising ground, bounced high in the air, then skidded round sideways behind the hedge and stopped.

The first thing I did was to switch off all my lights. I am not quite sure what made me do this except that I knew that if you are hiding from someone in the dark you don't shine lights all over the place to show where you are. I sat very still in my dark car.

The hedge was a thick one and I couldn't see through it. The car had bounced and skidded sideways in such a way that it was now right off the track. It was behind the hedge and in a sort of field. It was facing back towards the filling-station, tucked in very close to the hedge. I could hear the police car. It had pulled up about fifty yards down the road and now it was backing and turning. The road was far too narrow for it to turn round in one go. Then the roar from the motor got louder and he came back fast with the engine revving and the headlamps blazing.

from **Danny, the Champion of the World**
by Roald Dahl

On the run!

Read the extract on page 72, then answer these questions in complete sentences.

A
1. Why did Danny think the police car would stop?
2. What was Danny's "only thought"?
3. Where did he hide?
4. Why could he not see the police car from his hiding place?

B
1. Which part of the story did you find the most exciting? Why?
2. Which words or phrases make it exciting?
3. Do you think Danny behaved sensibly in hiding? Give reasons for your answer.

Pronouns

A **pronoun** is a word which stands in place of a noun:

Kath loves writing stories.   **She** loves writing stories.

Kath and Paul found a **silver ring**.   **They** found **it**.

Pronouns can be singular: I, me, you, he, she, it, him, her.
Or they can be plural: we, us, they, them.

A Write out these sentences. Underline the pronouns.
1. He went with me to the shops.
2. They finished it before school.
3. She bought him a present.
4. He thanked her and opened it.
5. We will meet you tomorrow.
6. She gave them back to us.

B Rewrite these sentences, changing the **emphasised** words to suitable pronouns.
1. **Kath** told **Jan** a story.
2. **Kate and Sangita** gave **the money** to Jake.
3. **The dog** barked at **the girl**.
4. **Matthew** gave the book to **my brother and me**.

C Rewrite these sentences, replacing the **emphasised** words with suitable pronouns.
1. After Narinder and I finished our work **Narinder and I** went to the shops.
2. When Dan gave Leanne a book, **Leanne** thanked **Dan for the book**.
3. The Smith family were to have a picnic, but bad weather stopped **the Smith family** from having **a picnic**.

D Rewrite this passage, changing the **emphasised** words to suitable pronouns.

Sophie and Mel went to see Mr Knox. **Mr Knox** had a new puppy. **Sophie and Mel** played with **the puppy**. **Sophie and Mel** phoned their mum to tell her about **the puppy**. **Their mum** said **their mum** would come and see **the puppy** too.

What happens next?

Read again the passage on page 72 about Danny hiding from the police. Imagine you are in the car.

What would you do next? What might happen then? Plan your ideas for a story in one of these ways.

● Draw a storyboard.

● Make a flow chart of the key incidents.

| Danny is driving late at night to find his dad. |
⬇
| He is seen by a policeman in a police car. |

● Make a list of exciting words to include in your writing. Think of words to describe what you see and hear, and how you feel.

Begin your writing with this sentence:

The police car came back fast, headlamps blazing.

First, second and third person pronouns

Pronouns may be in the first, second or third person:

	Singular	*Plural*
First person	I, me	we, us
Second person	you	you
Third person	he, she, it, him, her	they, them

A Rewrite these sentences, changing the singular pronouns to plural.
1. I went with him to the match.
2. He bought it for me.
3. I packed it carefully.
4. I went with her.
5. She will meet you tomorrow.

B Use each of these pronouns in a sentence of your own: me, we, you, us, him, them, it, she, you, her.

The Great Mouse Plot

This is a true story written by Roald Dahl, about himself. He and the other schoolboys have found a dead mouse which Roald decides to put in a jar at the sweet shop.

"Make sure you put it into a jar which is used often," somebody said.

"I'm putting it in Gobstoppers," I said. "The Gobstopper jar is never behind the counter."

"I've got a penny," Thwaites said, "so I'll ask for one Sherbet Sucker and one Bootlace. And while she turns away to get them, you slip the mouse in quickly with the Gobstoppers."

Thus everything was arranged. We were strutting a little as we entered the shop. We were the victors now and Mrs Pratchett was the victim. She stood behind the counter, and her small malignant pig-eyes watched us suspiciously as we came forward.

"One Sherbet Sucker, please," Thwaites said to her, holding out his penny.

I kept to the rear of the group, and when I saw Mrs Pratchett turn her head away for a couple of seconds to fish a Sherbet Sucker out of the box, I lifted the heavy glass lid of the Gobstopper jar and dropped the mouse in. Then I replaced the lid as silently as possible. My heart was thumping like mad and my hands had gone all sweaty.

"And one Bootlace, please," I heard Thwaites saying. When I turned round, I saw Mrs Pratchett holding out the Bootlace in her filthy fingers.

"I don't want all the lot of you troopin' in 'ere if only one of you is buyin'," she screamed at us. "Now beat it! Go on, get out!"

As soon as we were outside, we broke into a run. "Did you do it?" they shouted at me.

"Of course I did!" I said.

"Well done you!" they cried. "What a super show!"

I felt like a hero. I *was* a hero. It was marvellous to be so popular.

from **Boy** *by Roald Dahl*

Day 1

Bottled mouse

Read the extract on page 75, then answer these questions in complete sentences.

A
1. What was the Great Mouse Plot?
2. Whose job was it to distract Mrs Pratchett?
3. Why did she tell them to get out?
4. Why did the writer feel like a hero?

B
1. How did the writer feel as he entered the shop?
2. How did he feel as he left it?
3. What do you think of the boy's behaviour? Give a reason for your answer.

Day 2
S

Using speech marks

In written work spoken words are put inside speech marks.

● Put " before the first spoken word.

● Begin the first spoken word with a capital letter.

● Put a comma, full stop, question mark or exclamation mark after the last spoken word.

● Put " to show that the spoken words have ended.

ONE SHERBET SUCKER, PLEASE.

"One Sherbet Sucker, please," Thwaites said.

A Copy these sentences, putting speech marks around the spoken words.
1. Let's go skating, suggested Lisa.
2. What time are you going? she asked.
3. Would you like a piece of cake? asked Mum.
4. This is not easy, he complained.
5. I think it's going to rain again, I said.

B Copy these sentences, putting speech marks around the spoken words. Add commas and question marks where they are needed.
1. I'll see you after school Jane told him.
2. He said I think it's going to be hot.
3. How on earth did you do that he asked.

4. Jack said It's time I was leaving.
5. Fiona laughed and said That was really funny.
6. Has anyone phoned she asked.

C Complete these sentences with spoken words of your own. Put in speech marks, capital letters, commas and question marks where they are needed.
1. The police officer said
2. Dad said
3. Lee asked his friend
4. The girl whispered

Joining sentences

Join these sentences with **when**, **while** or **since.**
1. He hid the toy. He saw the teacher.
2. Sue is reading. She waits for her friend.
3. The flowers opened. The sun came out.
4. We decided not to go. It was raining.
5. He is much better. He went to see the doctor.
6. We will stop work. It gets dark.
7. Max washed up. Dad did the dusting.
8. The table shines. You polished it.

Write an extended story

You can write quite a long story if you share out the work among a team of writers, with each person writing just one chapter. Follow these steps:

Planning

Plan your story together, chapter by chapter, and in detail. The planning is most important as each writer will need to know what happens before and after his or her chapter.

Display the writing plan where everyone can see and refer to it.

Decide who will write which chapters. The first and last chapters are particularly important. Make a list of chapter numbers and writers so everyone is clear what they are doing.

Choose a small team of editors to read the chapters to check that the plan is being followed, and that there are no unexpected changes in character, plot or setting.

Writing

Plan your chapter in three paragraphs.

Read the story plan carefully up to the point where your chapter begins. The action in your first paragraph should follow on immediately from the end of the previous chapter.

Read the story plan for the chapter which follows yours. Your last paragraph should lead directly into it.

Think of a good title for your chapter.

Write your chapter.

Revising

Check to see that your chapter fits the story plan.

Make any improvements you think are needed.

Correct any spelling and punctuation errors.

Let the editorial team check your work.

Make any further changes that are necessary.

Publishing

Put the chapters into order.

Make them into a book, with a list of chapter titles and authors' names.

Prepare a front cover with an exciting illustration and title.

Write a back cover "blurb" saying what the story is about, and explaining how it was written.

A Snake in the Garden

The setting of this story is India. A young girl, Jazeera, goes into the garden to help the servant boy, Anil, deal with a snake. She notices a Frisbee lying on the grass.

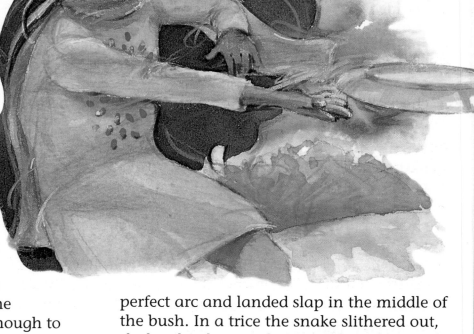

Jazeera's eye was caught by the bright yellow disc staring forgotten at the blue sky. They needed a distraction and that might just work. She whispered to Anil and pointed at the Frisbee. Anil tried to stop her, but it was no good. Jazeera tiptoed across the garden and gingerly picked up the hot plastic toy. She straightened up, her eyes fixed on the bush. The leaves rustled, and it wasn't the wind.

A sour taste poured into Jazeera's mouth. The taste of fear. Jazeera froze. She was sure that the thudding of her heart was loud enough to disturb a whole nest of vipers, but apart from the first rustle, the bush did not move. Gingerly, she inched backwards until she felt the reassuring presence of Anil behind her.

Jazeera and Anil stood on the edge of the lawn clutching their weapons. From the corner of her eye, Jazeera saw the worried figure of Nani at the bedroom window. She ignored it. Nothing must disturb her concentration now, or her aim. She mouthed the words silently at Anil:

"ONE …

TWO …

THREE."

With deadly accuracy the Frisbee left Jazeera's clammy hands, swooped in a perfect arc and landed slap in the middle of the bush. In a trice the snake slithered out, shaken by the attack. It was then that Anil dashed forwards bashing the ground with his stick and uttering blood-curdling yells.

The onslaught was more than the snake could handle. With surprising speed it shot across the garden, hardly seeming to touch the ground. It veered around the gate and out into the comparative peace of the road, chased by a still screaming Anil who slammed the gate firmly shut. The last Anil saw of the snake, it was heading off into a deserted building site at the end of the street.

Jazeera joined Anil at the gate and threw her arms around him in joyful relief. "You did it!" she cried.

*from **Jazeera in the Sun** by Lisa Bruce*

Day 1

Jazeera finds a Frisbee

Read the extract on page 78, then answer these questions in complete sentences.

A

1. How did Jazeera get the snake out of the bush?
2. What did Anil do then?
3. Where did the snake go?
4. What did Jazeera do then? How did she feel?

B

1. Do you think this could have happened in real life? What makes you think so?
2. Do you think what the children did was dangerous? Give a reason for your answer.
3. What might have happened if Jazeera had not helped Anil?

Day 2

Personal pronouns

Pronouns that stand in place of a person's name are called **personal pronouns**:

I, you, he, she, it, we, they, me, him, her, us, them.

Anil joined Jazeera at the gate. **He** joined **her** at the gate.

Think for yourself what the missing personal pronouns are in this further extract from *Jazeera in the Sun*. Write one word for each space.

Anil grinned. He had done it and ___1___ would never have believed it possible. Still ___2___ wouldn't have been able to do it on ___3___ own.

"___4___ were great," ___5___ said enthusiastically.

Nani, Aunty and Jazeera's mother ran down to the gate and hugged Jazeera, telling ___6___ what a brave, naughty, silly girl ___7___ had been. Jazeera looked up to see tears in ___8___ mother's eyes.

"What's wrong?" ___9___ asked.

" ___10___ might have been killed, Jazeera."

Possessive pronouns

Pronouns which show that something belongs to someone are called **possessive pronouns**: mine, yours, his, hers, ours, theirs.

This book is **mine**, that one is **yours**.

A Copy and complete these sentences with possessive pronouns.
1. These pens belong to us. They are _____.
2. The coat belongs to you. It is _____.
3. The ball belongs to Ali. It is _____.
4. Jazeera owns the Frisbee. It is _____.
5. This is the Smiths' house. It is _____.

B Copy and complete these sentences with suitable possessive pronouns.
1. This belongs to me. It is _____.
2. This ball is _____ but that one is _____.
3. Our car is fast, but _____ is faster.
4. These books are _____.
5. _____ are over there.

Days 3 and 4

A snake in the garden

Anil has spotted a snake in the garden of a house in India. It has slithered into a bush and Jazeera has gone to help him deal with it.

Imagine you are Jazeera or Anil. Tell the story of the snake in the garden from your point of view.

1. What is Jazeera thinking? Why is Anil trying to stop her?

2. How does Jazeera feel? What is she thinking?

3. How do Jazeera and Anil feel now?

4. How does Anil feel? What might Jazeera be thinking?

5. Why is Anil screaming?

6. How do Jazeera and Anil feel now?

Plan your work like this:

Paragraph 1 (pictures 1 and 2)
Tell the reader where the story is set. Explain why you think there is a snake in the bush.

Paragraph 2 (pictures 3, 4 and 5)
What happens when the Frisbee is thrown? Say how you feel.

Paragraph 3 (picture 6)
What happened after the snake had been chased out of the garden? How do you feel now?

Day 5

Homonyms

Homonyms are words with the same spelling but different meanings.

He was startled by a **jet**.

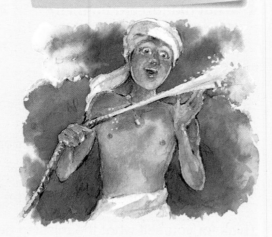

A Which meaning of the **emphasised** word fits these sentences?
1. He filled in the **form**.
   a) a class in a school
   b) a paper with questions and spaces for answers
2. I hope to be fit for Saturday's **match**.
   a) an organised game
   b) a stick of wood used to make a flame

B Use each of these words in two sentences to show two different meanings: cup, roll, seal, stamp, light.

The Library

The books in a library are arranged in two groups: fiction and non-fiction.

Fiction books are stories about people and events which have been invented by the author.

Non-fiction books give facts and information about people, places and things.

Fiction books

To find a fiction book we need to know who wrote it, because fiction books are placed on the shelf according to the first letter of the author's surname. Joan Aiken books are on shelf A, Leila Berg on shelf B, and so on through the alphabet.

Non-fiction books

Non-fiction books are grouped in topics.

Look at this topic web:

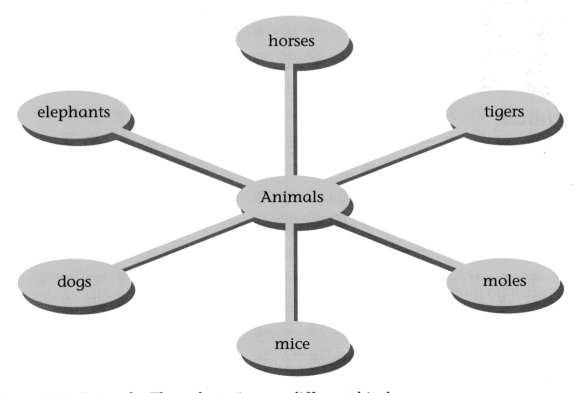

The main topic is Animals. The sub-topics are different kinds of animals. You would find books on these topics on the Animals shelf.

Fiction and non-fiction

Read page 81, then answer these questions in complete sentences.

A
1. What are fiction books?
2. What are non-fiction books?
3. What do we need to know to find a fiction book?
4. Fiction books are arranged according to the author's _____.

B
1. What main topics would have these as sub-topics?
   a) Venus, Earth, Jupiter, Mercury
   b) chaffinch, eagle, ostrich, parrot
2. Suggest three sub-topics for each of these:
   a) fish
   b) transport
   c) famous people

Fiction books

A Put this list of fiction authors into alphabetical order:

Robert Westall	Anthony Browne	Pippa Goodheart	Bernard Ashley
Jenny Nimmo	Rosemary Sutcliff	Roald Dahl	Margaret Mahy
Kathryn Cave	Hazel Townson	Jan Mark	Mark Haddon

B Put this list of fiction authors into alphabetical order:

Alan Gibbons	Norma Clarke	Adele Geras	Charles Ashton
Caroline Castle	Linda Hoy	Alan Snow	Dick King-Smith
Allan Ahlberg	Robert Swindells	Jenny Koralek	Ann Halam

Making notes

Read this passage and then answer the questions on the right:

Some food can only be grown in a particular climate. Rice needs lots of rain. Oranges and bananas grow in hot countries, but apples and pears grow in cooler climates. People who grow food in one country trade with other countries so that they can eat different kinds of food.

Fresh food can go bad very quickly, but there are lots of ways in which we can make it last longer. Freezing food can keep it fresh for many months. Fish, meat and peas are often bought frozen. Food can be put into cans, which are then sealed and heated. Favourite canned foods are baked beans and tomatoes. Canned food can be kept for years. Foods such as rice, pasta and flour are dried to make them last longer. Pickling in vinegar is a way of preserving foods such as onions.

A
1. What is the main idea of paragraph 1?
2. What is the main idea of paragraph 2?
3. Pick out the key words in the text. Use them to write notes.

B Find books in your library to help you answer these questions:
1. Where does **coffee** come from?
2. Why is **Florence Nightingale** famous?
3. Name three **cities** in **France**.
4. What kind of **animal** is a **wallaby**?
5. What are the names of the **planets** in the **solar system**?

Make your own information book

A Use books in your library to help you make an information book of your own.

Look for books on one of these topics:

Birds   Reptiles   Pets   Fish

Each book will have a number of sub-topics. Choose just **four** sub-topics and make a list. For instance:

Pets: cats, hamsters, dogs, gerbils

Make notes on each the four sub-topics you have listed, using these headings to help you:

Description

Habitat (where it lives)

Food

Use your notes to write your information book:
a) Put your sub-topics in alphabetical order.
b) Write a page about each sub-topic.
c) Make a contents list for your book.
d) Make an index.
e) Design a cover with a title, your name as the author and an eye-catching illustration.
f) Write a back-cover "blurb" describing what your book is about.

B Make an information book on a subject you are especially interested in, such as a sport or a hobby.

Jacqueline Hyde

Jacqueline Good is a well-behaved girl: polite, punctual, clean, tidy and helpful. Then one day she finds an old medicine bottle in Grandma's attic.

There was some stuff in it. Thickish liquid that moved like treacle. There wasn't much – about two centimetres. The cork had been pushed so far in I couldn't get a grip so I took it under the skylight and worked at it with my nails, and after a bit I got it out.

It came away with a pop. I sniffed it but it just smelt old so I sniffed the bottleneck. It smelt sort of sharp. Fruity. Bit like lime juice. It made my nostrils tingle, and the tingle seemed to pass behind my eyes into my forehead and then spread across the inside of my skull till it reached the nape of my neck and trickled down my spine.

It's hard to describe how it made me feel, and you wouldn't believe me anyway. I felt … excited. I was bursting with energy, like Popeye after a spinach fix. Ready for anything.

There was this mirror. A flyspecked full-length mirror that swivelled in a frame. I looked at myself. I thought I'd look different but I didn't so I stuck my tongue out. "Just look at you," I sneered. "You're so *good*, aren't you, Jacqueline Hyde? So yuckily, sick-makingly good. See how *clean* you've kept yourself, even in this mucky old attic. Grandma *will* be pleased."

I hated my reflection. *Hated* it. I know it sounds daft but I did. There was a flatiron on the floor. A rusty flatiron. I bent down and grabbed it and snarled, "Here, Jacqueline Good – catch." I got that mirror dead-centre and it shattered, spraying glittering fragments everywhere. The iron rebounded and crashed on the dusty floorboards and I heard Grandma call out, "Jacqueline – what's happening up there? Are you all right?"

Oh, I was all right, all right. *More* than all right. For the first time in my life I was *alive*. Fully alive. I headed for the door.

*from **Jacqueline Hyde** by Robert Swindells*

In the attic

All the missing words are adjectives.

First read the extract on page 84, and then look at the extract below, which describes what happens just before Jacqueline finds the bottle.

Think for yourself what the missing words are. Write one word for each space.

There was no ___1___ light up there. All there was was one ___2___ skylight in the slope of the roof. I found the binliner straightaway. It was by the door. I left it there and started poking about. There was ___3___ furniture, ___4___ household gadgets and tea-chests full of crockery, ___5___ glassware and ___6___ clothes. There were ___7___ things on the floor to trip you up – piles of ___8___ magazines, ___9___ flatirons and ___10___ vases. There was one roller skate. I'm not kidding – one. It must have belonged to Long John Silver or somebody. And a jam jar crammed with paint-brushes, and some stair rods and a pram and a handbag and a wire birdcage with a ___11___ budgie in it. I nearly crouched down and said who's a ___12___ boy then?, but I was frightened of getting my frock ___13___.

Compound words

A **compound word** is a word made by joining two shorter words.

A Make a list of all the compound words in the text extract above.

skylight, ...

B Use each word from your list in a sentence of your own.

Homonyms

Homonyms are words which have the same spelling but different meanings.

A Use each of the following words in two sentences of your own to show two different meanings.
1. hard
2. iron
3. right
4. spell
5. cross

B Use each of the following words in three sentences of your own to show three different meanings.
1. pass
2. good
3. fine
4. even
5. trunk

Looking for fun

The story of Jacqueline Hyde continues …

Grandma was at the foot of the stairs. "You've been ever such a long time dear," she said as I started down. "And what was that awful noise?"

"What noise?" I said, "I didn't hear anything."

"It was a loud thump," she said, "like something heavy falling over. You *must* have heard it."

"No." I brushed past her with a straight face but laughing inside and she said, "You've forgotten the bag."

I shook my head. "I didn't forget, Gran." She hates being called Gran. "You can get it yourself – the exercise'll be good for your rheumatism."

Outside, the rain had stopped. I turned left and set off walking. It must've been magic, the stuff in that bottle. My mind was fantastically sharp. Colours seemed unnaturally bright. I was seeing things I wouldn't normally notice, like the way the sun glistened on the flagstones, walls and railings, and how puddles reflected bits of duck-egg blue. There were smells too – wet leaves and a whiff of some faraway bonfire, and I could feel sensations such as the breeze on my cheek and the rub of my shirt against my skin. When I breathed in, the cold air filled my lungs like silver light. I felt cool, strong and fearless as I motored on down, looking for fun.

Now imagine **you** are Jacqueline Hyde. You have sniffed the old medicine bottle in the loft and have changed into the very opposite of the well-behaved person you once were. Write about what happens next. How will you behave? What will the consequences be?

Think about how the bottle has changed the way you feel:

- Colours are very bright, and you can see things you wouldn't normally see.

- Your sense of smell is very sharp.

- You have a greater sense of touch: you can feel sensations such as the breeze on your cheek and the rub of your shirt against your skin.

- You feel strong and fearless.

- You are looking for mischief.

- You say exactly what you want to say, without worrying about offending people.

Write as if you were talking to a friend. Use shortened forms of words such as wasn't, didn't, etc.

Plan your story in three paragraphs:

Paragraph 1
What sort of mischief will you get up to?

Describe what you do, how you feel and how others react.

Paragraph 2
Describe what happens as the effects of the bottle wear off. How different do you feel now?

What are the consequences of your actions? What regrets do you have?

Paragraph 3
How does it all end?

Joining sentences

We can join sentences by using a conjunction such as **so**, **if** or **though**.

It was a hot day. We decided to swim. It was a hot day **so** we decided to swim.

We might go swimming. It is hot today. We might go swimming **if** it is hot today.

We went swimming. It was cold. We went swimming **though** it was cold.

A Join these sentences with **so**, **if** or **though**.
1. The dog will bite him. He annoys it.
2. He climbed the wall. It was dangerous.
3. He wasn't looking. He tripped.
4. He took his time. He was told to hurry.
5. We'll have time for a drink. We arrive early.
6. He began to laugh. He tried not to.

B Join these sentences with **so**, **if** or **though**.
1. He's working now. He can rest later.
2. We'll play inside. It is too wet.
3. He won't win the race. He doesn't train hard.
4. She was sad. I cheered her up.
5. She wrapped up well. She would not get cold.
6. You will be late. You do not hurry.

C Make up three sentences of your own, using **so**, **if** and **though**.

A Sudden Glow of Gold

Toby has just rediscovered a lamp under his bed. It was given to him by his sister Sophie.

Toby reached under the bed, and drew the old lamp out into the light. Funny. He hadn't noticed before it had such delicate tracery around the handle and up the little spout. And it was heavier than he remembered. Perhaps it was made of real brass.

Toby gave it a rub.

At first, nothing happened. The dingy metal looked just as dull and rusty as before.

Toby rubbed harder.

"Abracadabra!" he muttered to himself, without thinking. "Abracadabra!" He was so taken up with his rubbing that he didn't notice a long golden fingernail creeping silently over his shoulder.

"Abracadabra!" crooned Toby. "Abracadabra!"

A sudden glow of gold was filling the room. The air warmed, wafting the scent of flowers over his head, and there was a ripple of birdsong.

He still didn't notice. He just kept on rubbing.

"Abracadabra!" he sang merrily. "Abracadabra!"

The long golden fingernail poked Toby hard.

Dropping the lamp in fright, Toby spun round.

A genie, clothed in gold, was standing there watching him through narrowed eyes. The finger that had poked Toby's shoulder was still stretched out threateningly towards him. The golden nail glittered and the genie's eyes flashed.

"Stones of the desert have sharper ears than my master!"

Now, even through his terror, Toby heard the birdsong and smelled the warm scents, and noticed the golden glow flooding his bedroom.

He couldn't speak. He was too astonished. And far too scared to think of anything to say.

It didn't matter. The genie obviously had a lot to get off his golden chest.

"Any fool knows that it is easier to build two palaces than keep one tidy. But never in all my thousand years have I endured a resting place so like the lair of a jackal."

Toby couldn't help it. The words popped out.

"But you came from Sophie Hunter's room! That's far worse!"

from **A Sudden Glow of Gold**
by Anne Fine

Toby rubs the lamp

Read the extract on page 88, then answer these questions in complete sentences.

A

1. What had Toby not noticed about the lamp before?
2. Why did he not realize that a genie had appeared?
3. What made him finally realize?
4. What did the genie think of Toby's room?

B

1. Describe how the room changed as Toby rubbed the lamp.
2. Why did Toby mention Sophie's room?
3. Do you think this story could really happen? What makes you think so?

Reading for clues

Think for yourself what the missing words are in this further extract from *A Sudden Glow of Gold*. Write one word for each space.

The genie's lip curled at the memory, and just for a ___1___ a picture swam into Toby's mind of this ___2___ standing in Sophie's room amongst all the crumpled ___3___ wrappers, the mugs of cold tea with fungus ___4___ the top – and *worse*. It was a strange vision, ___5___ everything about this genie looked so golden and perfect, ___6___ the coiled gold turban on his head to ___7___ curving gold slippers on his feet. And had ___8___ dipped his fingernails in gold, or was he ___9___ so magical that parts of him were not even ___10___ and blood, but made of the most precious ___11___? The genie looked so polished, so glistening, you'd ___12___ he'd be grateful to be safely ___13___ from the horrors of Sophie Hunter's ___14___.

Words which signal time

A Write instructions on how to use a magic lamp. Write a sentence for each picture, beginning with the time word given.

First …   At the same time …   Then …   When …   Then …

The genie of the lamp

Write your own story about a genie and a magic lamp.

Plan your work like this:

Beginning
Where do you find the lamp?

What does it look like?

What happens when you rub it?

What does the genie look like?

What does the genie say?

Middle
What do you ask the genie to do?

What adventures do you have?

End
How does it all end?

Make your ending interesting. Stories which turn out to be a dream are very disappointing!

What is your wish, O Master?

Who dares summon the genie of the lamp?

The apostrophe in short forms

When people speak they use short forms of some words. The **apostrophe**, or raised comma, shows us where one or more letters have been missed out.

It's = it is   aren't = are not   couldn't = could not   won't = will not

A Write the full form of these:
1. I'm
2. he's
3. they're
4. we've
5. she's
6. couldn't
7. you've
8. wouldn't

B Write the short form of these:
1. could not
2. would not
3. should not
4. have not
5. cannot
6. do not
7. did not
8. will not
9. is not
10. are not

Hi, I'm Jeannie!

Do I have to?

C Use each of these short forms in a sentence of your own:
shouldn't, won't, couldn't, wouldn't, haven't.

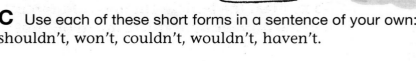

Unit 29

Word Puzzles

Riddles

A house full, a hole full,
You cannot catch a bowlful.

Round as a biscuit;
Busy as a bee;
Prettiest little thing
You ever did see.

Runs all day and never walks,
Often murmurs, never talks.
It has a bed, but never sleeps,
It has a mouth, but never eats.

Riddle me! Riddle me! What is that:
Over your head and under your hat?

Little Nancy Etticoat
In a white petticoat
And a red rose.
The longer she stands,
The shorter she grows.

Strange but True

I saw a fishpond all on fire
I saw a house bow to a squire
I saw a parson twelve feet high
I saw a cottage near the sky
I saw a balloon made of lead
I saw a coffin drop down dead
I saw two sparrows run a race
I saw two horses making lace
I saw a girl just like a cat
I saw a kitten wearing a hat
I saw a man who saw these too
And said though strange they all were true.

Anon

Wild Flowers

"Of what are you afraid, my child?"
inquired the kindly teacher.
"Oh, sir! the flowers, they are wild," replied
the timid creature.

Peter Newell

Thomas a Tattamus took two T's
To tie two tups to two tall trees,
To frighten the terrible Thomas a Tattamus!
Tell me how many T's there are in all **that**?

Can you find the answers?

Read the word puzzles on page 91 and then answer these questions in complete sentences.

A
1. What two kinds of tongue is the first riddle about?
2. Copy one of the riddles in your best writing. Write its answer.
3. What are the two meanings of "wild" in "Wild Flowers"?
4. What is the answer to the Thomas a Tattamus riddle?

B
1. What is a pun?
2. Explain the pun in the second riddle.
3. Explain the puzzle in "Strange But True".

W

Day 2

More homonyms

Find these words in your dictionary. Write sentences of your own to show two possible meanings for each word.

1. rock   4. fan
2. wave   5. bat
3. train

A food crossword

Copy and complete this crossword net.

Clues across
1. dried grapes
3. a leafy salad plant
5. a spread of fruit preserved in sugar
7. sliced bread made brown by heating
9. a sour tasting liquid sprinkled on chips
11. bitter white crystals used to flavour food

Clues down
2. white grains which are boiled and eaten
4. oranges and _____
6. bread and _____
8. oval food with yolks inside
10. sweet white crystals used to flavour food

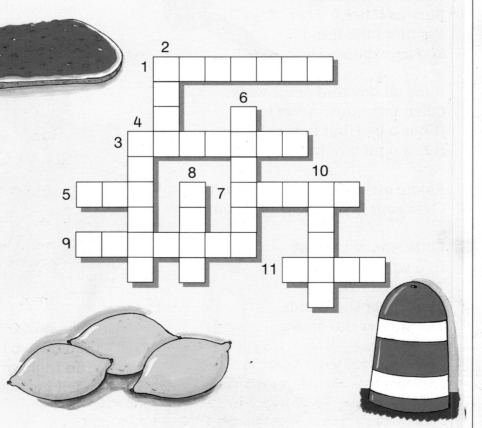

Write your own word puzzles

A Write your own clues for this crossword.
Use these headings: Clues across, Clues down.

2							9	
1 e	m	p	t	y			t	
l						8	i	
3 e	x	e	r	c	i	s	e	
p	4		6			e		
5 h	e	l	p	f	u	l		
a	o		l			l		
7 n	a	s	t	y		e		
t	s					r		

B A **pun** is a play on words. Explain the pun in this riddle.

What is the best cure for water on the brain?
A tap on the head.

C Use the two meanings of these words to complete the riddles.

1. **set**
   a) to become solid   b) to go below the horizon at dusk

   Why is the sun like jelly?
   Because _____

2. **lighter**
   a) not as heavy   b) not as dark
   Why was the box easier to carry at sunrise?
   Because _____

3. **fast**
   a) moving very quickly   b) showing a later time than the real time

   Why is the clock like a _____?
   Because _____.

D Make up some riddles with puns.

Find the homonym

A Find the homonym which links both meanings.

to split into pieces	_____	to stop for a short time before starting again
a metal	_____	to press out creases in clothes
to go underwater	_____	a large basin with taps
a kind of tree	_____	grey powder left when wood has burned
a small clock	_____	to look at for some time
a series of animal footprints	_____	a narrow path
one of the seasons	_____	a place where water comes from the ground
clever	_____	having a fine point or edge
to rub an itch	_____	a small cut
a place where money is made	_____	a plant whose leaves are used in cooking

B Write a tongue-twister like "Thomas a Tattamus":
a verse where almost all the words begin with the same sound.
Then try reading your tongue-twister as fast as you can
without tripping over your tongue! Try it out on your friends.

Unit 30

Letters

This unit looks at letters of different kinds. The style of each letter varies according to its purpose and audience.

16 Kensington Drive,
Morwick Green,
W. Yorks
7th April

Dear Sam,

I hope you are enjoying the holiday and everyone is well. Mum says to tell your mum that she'll be glad when we all go back to school, but then she would, wouldn't she?

Yesterday we had a wonderful trip to the National Museum of Photography, Film and Television in Bradford. They have an enormous cinema screen for special films called Imax. When I say enormous, I mean ENORMOUS! It's three stories high and when you're watching a film you can turn your head to look up, down and sideways. We saw a film called "Grand Canyon". It was like being there. I mean <u>really</u> being there. We were at the bottom of the canyon and you could look up and see the canyon rim high above you. It was incredible! You really must come over soon and I'll take you.

That's all I've time for now. Dad says I've got to tidy up my room. I suppose that means pushing more stuff under the bed!

See you soon,
Best wishes,
Danny

14 Mayfield
Drive,
Nutford,
Wessex
6ZZ 9PDQ
23rd September

Dear Sir/Madam,

I bought my son a Megaplay video game console for his birthday. At first he enjoyed playing with it, but it has now developed a quite annoying fault. Part way through a game the screen goes blank and the only way he can continue is to switch off and start again. As you will appreciate, this takes away all the fun.

In view of this I would like a replacement console, or my money back.

Yours faithfully,

Keith Pratt

14 Cross St,
Calbury,
Anyshire
ANY 36XX
10th August

Dear Jo,

Just a quick line to congratulate you on passing your exams. I knew you could do it. Well done!

I'll be up at the weekend to congratulate you personally, when I just might have a little treat for you!

Love,

Aunty Karen

EDITOR – I am writing in response to F.J.'s letter regarding the danger spot at the junction of Oxford Avenue and Cambridge Crescent. I live at that very junction and have witnessed one serious accident and several near misses. In every case it is the speed of the cars that is the problem. Drivers use this route as a shortcut, but it was never intended to carry so much traffic. I think speed bumps should be installed immediately.

P. Jones

Different kinds of letters

Look at the letters on page 94, then answer these questions.

A

1. Write Danny's address in your best writing.
2. Who has passed an exam?

3. What was Keith Pratt's complaint?
4. What does P. Jones want to see happen?

B Write a short reply to Aunty Karen's letter.

First, second and third person

A first person account is someone writing about himself or herself. It uses the pronouns **I** or **we**.

A third person account is about someone else.
It uses the pronouns **he**, **she** or **they**.

The second person is used when giving instructions or directions.

A Change this first person account by Nina into a third person account.

I went to a Summer Fair at school with my friend, Tina. We watched a police dog display, and then we threw wet sponges at Mr Ryan, our head teacher. My first sponge hit him right on the nose! Later I won a teddy bear on the tombola. We had a great time. I'm looking forward to the Christmas Fair.

Begin: *She went to a Summer Fair at school with her friend, Tina.*

B Change this third person account into a first person account.

Tom walks to school every Wednesday, but his mother picks him up in the car after school. Then they go to Grandma's for tea. She always gives him a slice of his favourite chocolate cake. After tea he goes to the library with his cousin Jack. Their favourite books are adventure stories.

Begin: *I walk to school ...*

C Change these second person instructions into a first person account.

Go down the road for about half a mile. Turn left at the post office and then first right. At the traffic lights turn right, and then right again immediately after the bridge. Go up the the hill and into the park. Wait by the fountain.

Begin: *I went down the road ...*

D Write a letter to a friend saying what you did yesterday.

Write your own letters

Write letters using some of these ideas.

a) You see an advertisement advertising a new toy catalogue from the Fawlty Toy Company. Write a letter asking for a catalogue and price list.

b) You have ordered a new toy from the Fawlty Toy Company, but they send you the wrong one, and it arrives damaged. Write a letter of complaint.

c) Write a note to a friend in another class asking for help with your work.

d) Write a letter to a relative about something you have enjoyed doing at school, or about an interesting place you have visited.

e) Write a letter to an author whose books you have enjoyed.
    Here are some things you might like to write about:
– Say why you enjoy his/her books.
– Say which is your favourite and why.
– Ask questions about the author and how he or she writes.
– You might also enclose your own book review of one of his or her books.

● When writing a letter to someone whose name you know, use the name in your greeting: **Dear Mrs Jennings,** or **Dear Sam.** End these letters with **Yours sincerely,** or, if it is a friend or relative, end in a more personal way: **Your loving nephew, Love from,** etc.

● When writing to someone whose name you do not know, begin in one of these ways: **Dear Sir, Dear Madam,** or **Dear Sir or Madam**. End these letters with **Yours faithfully.**

● Write your letters in paragraphs. Put each separate subject in a paragraph of its own.